The Hamburg Plays

Martin Crimp was born in 1956. His play *Attempts on Her Life* (1997) established his international reputation. His other work for theatre includes *When We Have Sufficiently Tortured Each Other*, *In the Republic of Happiness*, *Play House*, *The City*, *Fewer Emergencies*, *Cruel and Tender*, *The Country*, *The Treatment*, *Getting Attention*, *No One Sees the Video*, *Play with Repeats*, *Dealing with Clair* and *Definitely the Bahamas*. He is also the author of three texts, *Into the Little Hill*, *Written on Skin* and *Lessons in Love and Violence*, for operas by George Benjamin. His many translations of French plays include works by Genet, Ionesco, Koltès, Marivaux and Molière. *Writing for Nothing*, a collection of fiction, short plays and texts for opera, was published by Faber & Faber in 2019.

MARTIN CRIMP

The Hamburg Plays

The Rest Will Be Familiar to You from Cinema

Men Asleep

FABER & FABER

First published in 2019
by Faber and Faber Limited
The Bindery, 51 Hatton Garden
London EC1N 8HN
Typeset by Country Setting, Kingsdown, Kent CT14 8ES
Printed in England by by CPI Group (UK) Ltd, Croydon CR0 4YY

A CIP record for this book
is available from the British Library

ISBN 978-0-571-35398-9

MIX
Paper | Supporting
responsible forestry
FSC® C013604

Printed and bound in the UK on FSC® certified paper in line with our continuing
commitment to ethical business practices, sustainability and the environment.
For further information see faber.co.uk/environmental-policy

Our authorised representative in the EU for product safety is
Easy Access System Europe, Mustamäe tee 50, 10621 Tallinn, Estonia
gpsr.requests@easproject.com

4 6 8 10 9 7 5 3

Contents

Introduction

Leave the central station by the Kirchenallee exit, and to the left, diagonally opposite, across a broad but not very busy street, are the whitish façade and high flat dome of Deutsches Schauspielhaus Hamburg, the theatre which commissioned and produced the two plays in this volume.

The first – *The Rest Will Be Familiar to You from Cinema* – is a rewriting of Euripides' *Phoenician Women*, in which the eponymous Chorus of women, trapped in Thebes at a crucial moment of civil war, has been replaced by a group of 'girls' – young women, who, Sphinx-like, pose a string of unanswerable questions even as they drive through the action to its brutal conclusion: the banishment of Oedipus and Antigone's bitter conflict with Creon over the burial of her brother.

The second play – *Men Asleep* – is a different kind of experiment, based on two separate thefts. The title is stolen from a painting, *Schlafende Männer*, by the Austrian artist Maria Lassnig; and the self-destructing scenario of two couples meeting late at night, the younger on the territory of the older, from Albee's 1962 play *Who's Afraid of Virginia Woolf?* What might happen, I asked myself, if Albee's scenario was forced to encounter Lassnig's tender image?

Writing for a German theatre means writing for a resident company of actors. In *The Rest Will Be Familiar* a core group from the company was expanded by ten or so young actors still at drama school to play the 'girls'. Five years later I wrote *Men Asleep* for four specific members of this same company: Paul Herwig, Julia Wieninger, Josefine Israel and Tilman Strauss.

vii

I would like to take this opportunity to thank Katie Mitchell for introducing me to the theatre and for her part in instigating this work, as well as staging it. My thanks too to artistic director Karin Beier for her faith in scheduling these two plays before they were even written.

MC, November 2018

THE REST WILL BE FAMILIAR TO YOU FROM CINEMA

(ALLES WEITERE KENNEN SIE AUS DEM KINO)

after Euripides'
Phoenician Women

The Rest Will Be Familiar to You from Cinema, in a
German translation by Ulrike Syha, as *Alles Weitere
kennen Sie aus dem Kino*, was first performed at
Atelier 9/10, Studio Hamburg, on 24 November 2013,
transferring to the main stage of Deutsches Schauspielhaus
Hamburg in April 2014.

Jocasta Julia Wieninger
Antigone Sophie Krauß
Minder Ruth Marie Kröger
Polynices Bastian Reiber
Eteocles Christoph Luser
Kreon Paul Herwig
Teiresias Michael Wittenborn
Teiresias' Daughter Gala Winter
Menoecius Uwe Dreysel
Wounded Officer Niklas Bruhn
Softly-Spoken Officer Giorgio Spiegelfeld
Oedipus Jan-Peter Kampwirth
Girls Mieke Biendara, Katharina Bintz, Frederike Bohr,
  Tinka Fürst, Josephine Gehlhaar, Gesa Geue,
  Mersiha Husagic, Ruth Marie Kröger, Johanna Link,
  Rébecca Marie Mehne, Meike Schmidt, Tamara
  Theisen, Gala Winter

Direction Katie Mitchell
Set Design Alex Eales
Costumes Laura Hopkins
Music Paul Clark
Lighting James Farncombe
Sound Donato Wharton
Dramaturg Jörg Bochow

Characters

Jocasta
wife and mother of Oedipus

Antigone
daughter of Oedipus and Jocasta

Minder

Polynices
son of Oedipus and Jocasta

Eteocles
son of Oedipus and Jocasta

Kreon
Jocasta's brother

Teiresias
a prophet

Teiresias' Daughter
a child

Menoecius
Kreon's son, a child

Wounded Officer

Softly-Spoken Officer

Oedipus

and a number of
Girls

Scene

Interior of a large decaying house

—— If Carolin has three apples and Luise has
      three apples
how many oranges has Sabine got?
If Anna has two more ponies than Miriam
and Miriam's cat Bobby has seven kittens
then what is it like to kill?

—— Yes what is it like to kill
and what is it like to *be* Bobby the cat?

—— If a stone weighing seventy-five grams
travelling at two hundred kilometres per hour
can shatter a human pelvis
why are we all so beautiful?

—— Plus what is the value of x
if I stand here naked? Well?

Pause.

What is a Sphinx?
Why does a Sphinx kill?

—— What does a Sphinx want plus
who does a Sphinx fuck when?
Why is the Sphinx girls
and why are we all so beautiful?
What d'you think?

—— What d'you think of my hair?

—— Yes what d'you think of my hair
when I do *this* with it?

—————   Oh and why when the camera
          moves through the green tree-tops of Thebes
          at the end of the 1967 film of *Oedipus* by
              Pier Paolo Pasolini
          do you feel that you want to cry?
          Is it the music?

—————   Is it the music or is it because you're angry?
          Is it you're jealous of Silvana Mangano's
              dress?
          Or Silvana Mangano's mouth or hair?

—————   Who is this music by?
          Schubert? Is it by Mozart? Why do you want
              to cry?

—————   Why do you so much want to cry?
          And why do you resist crying?

          Accompanied on either side by two Girls,
          Jocasta appears in obscurity and is slowly led
          downstage. Music: the opening bars of
          Mozart K. 465.

—————   If two boys each pierced by a blade made of
              copper and tin
          take three hours to bleed to death
          in an ambient temperature of 30 degrees
              Celsius
          then who is this woman? Is she
          (a) mother of Oedipus?
          (b) wife of Oedipus?
          (c) mother of the two boys
          or (d) all of the above? Plus
          how can the dead live?

—————   Yes how can the dead live now?

8

Jocasta	Bright light. Time past.
Girl	Says Jocasta.
Jocasta	Says Jocasta.
Girl	Kadmos.
Jocasta	Kadmos – yes – leaves the Phoenician coast in search of Europe and eventually – she says – founds Thebes. He founds Thebes here where Thebes is now.
Girl	His fingers.
Jocasta	What?
Girl	His fingers.
Jocasta	His fingers – from the perpetual cracking open of shellfish to obtain dye – says Jocasta – smell of sex. *Pause.* He brings with him from the east bright light, the blood-red dye that's made him rich his own human material and the alphabet.
Girl	He marries.

Jocasta	He marries. Yes. He reproduces.
	Each new generation can now use his alphabet
	   to write.
	Each copies out the human material of the
	   one before

copies but corrupts the human material of
   the one before
until one day is born the unfortunate sum
of all these errors: Laios.
Laios marries.

Girl   Me.

Jocasta   What?

Girl   Marries me. Jocasta. Say it.

Jocasta   Laios marries me. Jocasta.

Pause.

We marry but we have no children.
Humiliated by his failure to reproduce
Laios visits the oracle at Delphi
where he pays the entrance fee and prays
   for a son
but Apollo says 'Don't do it.
Your own son will murder you plus
your whole family will go sliding across
   the palace floor
on a thin film of blood. End of interview.'
Laios comes home here to Thebes kicking
   up dust
and the moment he's through the door
   inserts his penis
into my vagina. 'This one's for Apollo,'
   he says.
It's my first orgasm.

Pause.

Bright light.
Time past.
Laios my husband is hunched over his
   work-bench

threading a steel rod through two holes
he's drilled in our newborn baby's ankles.
'Help me,' he says – 'I'm scared but I can't
   kill it.
Well don't just stand there staring,' he says,
'TAKE IT AWAY.'
Which is why eighteen years later
where two roads converge to make the letter Y
Laios – rushing back to Delphi this time
   to be reassured
the mutilated child he'd forced me to abandon
   didn't survive –
encounters – without knowing it – the
   child itself –
Oedipus – eighteen years old now –
and runs him off the road: 'HEY!'
The young man pulls out a butcher's knife
with an ash-wood grip and murders him.
My husband dead –

Pause.

Girl	I'm available.
Girl	I'm available – say it.
Jocasta	My husband dead, I'm available. Kreon my brother – says Jocasta – promises me to whoever can solve the – no.
Girl	Impossible question.
Jocasta	– impossible question – no.
Girl	Of the Sphinx.
Jocasta	– to whoever can solve the impossible question – no!
Girl	Of the Sphinx. SAY IT!

Jocasta	– promises me

Jocasta – promises me
to whoever can solve the impossible question
of the Sphinx.

Girl Good. Oedipus swaggers.

Jocasta Oedipus swaggers in. 'It's not difficult,'
he says
'The answer's a human being. Now make me
king.'

Pause.

Oh his clear eyes! His strong precise grip!
Yes with my own beautiful boy-husband
I have two more sons: Polynices, Eteocles,
and then Antigone, Ismene,
my two angry little girls.

Pause.

Time past.
Light dims.
Oedipus – older now – bangs open the
door one night
crawls into our high-up bed stinking of
blood and sweat.
'What's wrong?'
'Nothing. New information. Go back to sleep.'
Turns out on finding he's married to me –

Girl To his own mother.

Jocasta – to his own mother – yes –
he's used a hot needle to blind himself.
In the morning he won't stop screaming.

Pause.

Light dimmer still.
His own sons – look – are now dragging the
disgraced King

Oedipus my boy my husband
by his ankles up the stone stairs.
They want to shut him away in darkness
and share power for themselves.
'Don't think two fucked-up little shits like you
could ever share anything
unless you've split it apart with a knife first,'
    he goes.
They spit in his face – bang the door shut –

Girl   They've been cursed.

Jocasta They've been cursed – I know – yes –
by their own father.
'Don't panic,' says Polynices 'let's just
    separate.'
'Yes yes yes we'll separate,' says Eteocles
'I'll go away. You stay here.'
'No' says Polynices 'I'm the youngest, I'll
    go first
but look we should make it formal: let's say
    each of us will hold executive power over
    the city one year at a time
while the other keeps away.' 'Sure,' says
    Eteocles.
'Alternate years – whatever – where do
    I sign?'
But after year one's elapsed
and Polynices reappears on the doorstep
    relaxed and smiling
with presents for his sisters
Eteocles won't let him back.

Pause.

Bright light.
The time is now now.
Out there beyond the city walls Polynices

13

	– who rushed straight into a toxic political marriage – has assembled a vast army of violent men. For days and for days I've worked at engineering a truce so he can come here with immunity meet Eteocles and negotiate.
Girl	Why's he not here?
Jocasta	Why's he not here?
Girl	Has one of them broken the terms / of the truce?
Jocasta	Has one of them already broken the hard-won terms / of the truce?
Girl	All I can hear inside my head is my own son / screaming and screaming.
Jocasta	NO! DON'T KEEP TELLING ME WHAT TO SAY! I am free. I am free. I'm a human being. Look at me. I can say what I like. *Pause.*
Girl	Says Jocasta.
Jocasta	Says Jocasta, wife and mother of Oedipus.

SCENE THREE
ANTIGONE AND MINDER

*Antigone slips out of the room upstairs and encounters
her Minder. A Girl is squatting on the staircase, her back
to us perhaps.*

| **Minder** | I've been waiting. |

Antigone becomes self-conscious, says nothing.

I said I've been waiting.

Antigone   What do I say?

Girl   You scared me.

Antigone   What?

Girl   You scared me.

Antigone   You scared me.

Minder   You're late.

Antigone   What?

Minder   You're late.

Antigone   So?

Minder   You're late.

Pause. Antigone turns to the Girl for help. However. she doesn't find this stressful: for the moment it's a kind of game. The Girl mouths 'father'.

Antigone   I've been with my father.

Minder   I can see where you've been.
         What were you doing in there?

Antigone   He wanted to see my new skirt.

Minder   How could he 'see your skirt'?

Girl   Fingers.

Antigone   With his fingers of course.

Minder   Where's your sister?

Antigone   Ismene can't come. She's got music.

Minder	You know you're not meant to be in there.
Antigone	You're obsessed. He's my father. Well come on – you promised you'd show me 'the enemy'.

Pause.

(*Turns to Girl.*) Is this the stone?

Girl	No it's the kiss.
Antigone	The kiss?

Girl nods.

Well come on – you promised you'd show me
    'the enemy'.
Don't look so fierce. You promised.
Remember?

*She kisses the Minder. Confident that the
scene is progressing as it should, the Girl
withdraws. There's something prolonged and
over-intimate about the kiss. The Minder
tactfully separates herself.*

Minder	Well you need to get up on this. And please please please be careful.

*Some kind of chair or stool or ladder
arrangement is needed since standing at
floor level doesn't give a good enough view.
Antigone's reaction is one of excitement,
not fear.*

Antigone	Oh my god! There's hundreds of them!
Minder	Thousands. You're looking at upwards of ten thousand men.
Antigone	Ten thousand men. Amazing. All that metal.
Minder	It's bronze.

Antigone	Bronze – yes – copper and tin. Amazing.
	She looks.
	Weird.
Minder	What is?
Antigone	Look at those ones moving in groups. Ha. They're chasing their own shadows.
Minder	That's Special Forces.
Antigone	What's Special Forces?
Minder	Specially trained – they're looking for weaknesses.
Antigone	We don't have any weaknesses.
Minder	They'll still look.
Antigone	Why can't we kill them? I'd like to kill them now.
Minder	They're out of range.
Antigone	Ten thousand men. All that metal. It hurts my eyes.
Minder	Come over here.
Antigone	What?
Minder	Come here and look at this. Look at the trees.
	They move to a new viewing position.
Antigone	Ha. They've gone. What happened?
Minder	They've chopped them all down for firewood.
Antigone	That's horrible. But look! Look! I can see the river! It's all sparkly! And oh oh oh oh oh there's somebody in the water – look. Who's that crossing the river on a horse?

Minder	That's Tydéus.
Antigone	But that river is ours! It's ours! It's sacred!
Minder	Not to him.
Antigone	Tydéus? Not the one married to that bitch's sister?
Minder	Don't talk about women / like that.
Antigone	That bitch Polynices married. Why did he have to marry some thick little tight-arsed bitch?
Minder	Please don't say that.
Antigone	Oh but who is that boy? Look at his gold hair. He's beautiful.
Minder	Must be the Pretty One.
Antigone	(*laughs*) The Pretty One? Weird. What kind of name is that? His eyes are so dark. All black. Black black black – like honey. Oh my god!
Minder	What?
Antigone	He's looking right at us.
Minder	Move away.
Antigone	He's staring right at us. How dare he!
Minder	Move away.
Antigone	I'll teach him to stare. I'll kill him. I'll blind him. I want his head.
Minder	Please calm down. Where d'you think you're going? Antigone?
Antigone	(*laughing*) I want to see where my brother is.

Minder	(*also laughing in spite of herself*) Stop it. No. That is dangerous.
Antigone	Rubbish. I want to see Polynices.
Minder	Please be careful.

Antigone	So green.
	Look: there's sheep! What 're they doing?
	No – it's men – it's men making little piles
	    of stones.
	Why 're they making those little piles of
	    stones?

Minder	Sling-shot probably.
Antigone	Sling-shot – of course – how exciting. I can't see him. Is that him? – I don't know – it's all too bright – all those men, all that copper and tin – I wish I could fly down and touch him but which one is he? I'd land right next to my brother like a goddess – naked like Artemis – he'd be so surprised to see me naked! – d'you think he'd let me kiss him? – or would he be too afraid? – why are men all so cold and strange?
Minder	I want you to come down from there.
Antigone	Look: there's one with a machine.
Minder	It's dangerous.

Antigone	Look at his funny machine. I know who
	    that is: it's Kapanéus.
	He's really famous. He uses mathematics to
	    make machines.

Minder	Antigone.
Antigone	I like mathematics – it's like poetry – but not machines – unless poetry's really a machine –

but that's philosophy – I'm not sure I like philosophy: too many questions! – but where is my brother? – I so want to kiss him – why can't I? why can't I? – I just want wings – oh please give me wings and then I can –

With a loud crack a stone smashes at high velocity through a pane of glass.

Minder   Antigone!

Antigone   Oh shit! Oh shit!

Laughing with excitement and terror, Antigone makes her way back to the ground and lets the Minder hold her.

Amazing! That was amazing!

Minder   Are you hurt?

Antigone   Shit. What was it?

Minder   It was a stone.

Antigone   How can a stone do *that*?

Minder   Has it hurt you?

Antigone   Incredible. Incredible. I think I'm going to enjoy war.

Minder   (*with vehemence*) Don't be so stupid.

Antigone   *What* did you just say to me?

As Antigone coldly separates herself from her Minder, several of the Girls come forward and watch.

Minder   I'm sorry.

Antigone   Don't call me stupid. You're a slave.

Minder   I'm sorry.

Antigone First you got fucked then when they got sick
of fucking you they gave you a desk-job –
am I right? I said am I right?

Minder That's what happens to the side that loses –
yes.

Antigone What's that supposed to mean? This is Thebes.
I'm not *on* the side that loses. I can't be.

*Although she's still trembling, Antigone's
mood seems to lighten. She laughs again and
smoothes out her skirt.*

He said saffron-yellow with spots of red.
You don't have to look so hurt.

*A Girl has retrieved the stone and offers it
to Antigone, who takes it.*

One tiny stone. Amazing.

SCENE FOUR
GIRLS

—— If Sabine takes hold of a man's head
and pummels and pummels and pummels it
against the nose of a stone step
till the man's head bursts
then what does Luise want for Christmas?
 Make-up?
Or if Steffi has taken a tiny child –

—— Oh sweet!

—— – Yes taken a tiny child
whose face has been painted to look like a cat
and left it one metre from the cliff-edge
 blindfold

21

        then what is the meaning of justice? What's
            the test?

——   What's the test? Where's the needle?

——   Yes where is the long long needle
        you insert in the human cell
        to extract the human material
        and make sense of it? Did it snap?

——   Oh no!

——   Did the needle snap off in the human cell?

——   Oh no! Oh my god! How does that make
           you feel?
        Where is the sense in that?

——   Yes where is the sense? Where is the sense
        you expected to find deep in the / human cell?

——   Plus where is the world?

——   Yes where is the world now?
        What did you do? Select and click?
        Did you delete?

——   Oh no!

——   Did you select the world and delete it? Why?
        Where is the shop?

——   Where is the tree?

——   Where is the bright light? Where is the cinema?

——   Where are the comforting sirens of the police?
        Or the blackbird? Or the blackbird's egg?

——   Where's fresh coffee? Where is the cinema?
        What have you done
        with all those luminous reels of fiction –
        Grace Kelly – Stéphane / Audran?

——   Where are the comforting clouds of tear gas
       – the baton-charge – the magnificent horses?
       Should I be shaving my legs – yes or no?
       Are you satisfied?

——   Are you satisfied?

——   Are you really and truly / satisified?

——   Yes how satisfied exactly are you
       with the service you are receiving from us
           today
       and how would you rate that satisfaction
           out of ten
       when ten is extremely satisfied?

——   Write in black ink.

——   Use black ink only. Do not cross out.

——   If the answer's a human being
       then what is the question?

SCENE FIVE
POLYNICES AND GIRLS

Polynices Who are you?
            What are you doing here in my mother's
                house?
            I asked you a question.

Girl   We're the girls.

Polynices What girls?

Girl   Um . . . Phoenician girls.
            Don't hurt us. Look. We're innocent.

            The other Girls appear.

            We've come from the Phoenician coast

23

and we're on our way
to take up residence at –
where are we on our way
to take up / residence?

Girl   At Delphi.

Girl   Yes on our way – that's right –
to take up residence at Delphi
where we'll dance and dream for Phoebus
    Apollo
who is the god of prophecy and music.

Girl hums a little tune. Pause.

What? Don't you believe me?

Polynices   Why would I hurt you?

Girl   To prove that you're in control of course.

Polynices   I *am* in control.

Girl   Are you sure? Prove it. Hurt me. Go on.

She steps towards him. He backs away.

What's wrong?

Girl   Maybe he doesn't like Phoenician girls.

Girl   Maybe he doesn't like girls full stop.

The Girls laugh and surround him.

Polynices   I *am* in control.

*One of the Girls snatches a piece of paper
out of his pocket.*

Hey! Give that back!

The others gather round.

Girl   (*reads*) ' . . . (a) call off the army . . . (b)
refrain from . . . destruction of crops

24

(c) . . . refrain from scaling the walls . . .
(d) to restore and to maintain –'

Polynices I told you to give that back!

He grabs the Girl violently and forces her to release the paper. Some of the others scream. The Girl falls to the floor and struggles to breathe. Jocasta has been watching this.

Jocasta Move away from my son.
I said move away from my son.

Pause.

Polynices.
Look at you.
Let me touch your face.
Please don't be afraid of me.
I'm your mother – remember?
And this – says Jocasta – is your home.
Well say something.
Or kiss me at least.
That's right: kiss me. Like this.
Look and I'm going to put my arms
all the way round you
around and around you
plus put my head right here
next to your heart.

Polynices doesn't respond.

You're not the only one
angry with your brother.
It was an outrage.
And I need you to understand
it's not just your mother:
you have friends here
who long for you to come back.

He touches her hair.

Yes I cut off my hair –
was that too melodramatic? –
do I look strange? –
but I needed to make myself stop crying.
I needed to make the point
that a woman – however outraged –
need not scream and cry.
Oh and of course
when I caught your father upstairs
trying to hang himself
because of the so-called agony he feels
the tedious self-hatred and foreboding
he always feels about you two boys
I needed to take control.
Yes I removed his table and chair
so now – you'd laugh – he eats his meals
    on the floor.
And the funny thing is
he does seem much happier.

She moves away from him.

But you've married.
And into a different world – why?
What's wrong with our world here? Mmm?
You had a duty to make me happy –
to allow me to lead the procession
to allow me to fill the marriage-bath for you –
from your own city's sacred river
but you shut me out.
You shut out your own city.
You spat in its stream.
You left me standing here my darling in the
    dark
while you struggled to locate
your child-bride's vagina.
I hope it was worth it.

Polynices	Mother – I love my city
	but it has taken days of negotiation
	for me even to pass through the gate.
	You know that.
	I did not reject this city:
	I was forced out of it
	by a liar and a thief
	and to be camped out there in my own fields
	  like the enemy
	day after day is turning my mind inside-out.
	Those fields are my property.
	I've had to mutilate them with defensive
	  earthworks –
	hack down the olives – strip my own orchards
	  of fruit.
	The east meadow –
	says Polynices –
	where my father taught the two of us boys
	  to ride horses
	is the site now of stinking latrines.

Pause. She considers him.

What?

Jocasta	I need you to be rational.
Polynices	You think I'm not capable of putting my case?
Jocasta	Of course you're capable.
Polynices	You think I'm less capable than he is of putting my own case?
Jocasta	I said of course / you are capable.
Polynices	My wife is eleven years old. She sleeps in a separate building.

Some of the Girls react sceptically.

She sleeps in a separate building:
don't look at me like that.

Pause. Polynices close to tears.

Jocasta   (*gently*) And how did you persuade them
             to come here?

Polynices   Persuade who?

Girl   All these men – these / armies.

Jocasta   Yes all these men. What've you promised
             them?

Polynices   I've told you: I'm married now. We're family.
             They're obliged to come.

Jocasta   Yes but what've you promised them,
             Polynices?
             What is it they expect?

Polynices   Nothing. The normal things. Nothing.

Jocasta   And what are the normal things? Tell us.

Polynices   My brother has made this happen.
             You can't say I'm responsible.
             You know what the normal things are.
             Stop looking at / me like that.

Jocasta   (*glances at Girls*) I thought you were in
             control.

Polynices   I *am* in control
             but not in control of *this*.
             I don't *sleep*.
             You said a discussion – you said you could
             help – you said get my brother to talk – you
             said to me: put a case –

             *He sees Eteocles arrive and turns away in
             rage and frustration.*

– put a case – because I am perfectly capable
... yes I am perfectly capable ...

Pause.

Eteocles So. Good morning, Mummy. Good morning,
girls.
I'm here – says Eteocles –
doing – he says – precisely what Mummy
asked.
So I suggest that baby brother here starts
talking. Yes? No?
Come on: I'm a busy man – and unlike him
I have responsibilities towards my citizens.

Polynices They're not his citizens!

Jocasta Please. Calm down.
I need you – both of you – to control
yourselves.
You're rational human beings
so let's settle this – shall we? – through
rational debate.
This man isn't an animal, Eteocles,
he's your own brother and you will kindly
look at him.
I said: you will kindly look at him.
Thank you. And you – Polynices –
I want you to do the same.
Your brother is frightened and angry –

Eteocles That is complete / rubbish. No way – (*am
I frightened of him.*)

Jocasta Yes you are – don't deny it.
Everyone here's terrified. All night we can see
the fires out there burning and all day long
we can hear you sharpening steel.
We need clarity, Polynices.

You've come here with a foreign army.
You've laid siege to your own city.
I want you to explain to your brother –
    now – to his face –
what's forced you to take this extreme step.

Polynices hesitates.

(*Encouraging.*) Go on.

*Polynices gets out the sheet of paper the
Girls had snatched. A little awkwardly he
begins to read:*

Polynices   'Truth isn't complicated – and moral
    goodness –
as our own mother has always advised us –
    speaks for itself.
We had legitimate reasons for making our
    father abdicate.
But when he became aggressive
and attempted to poison the relationship
    between us
I left this house voluntarily – as my brother
    is well aware.
My principal aim in this was to spare my
    poor mother
further anxiety because I love her and
    sincerely believed
she had suffered enough.
We agreed that my brother would rule Thebes
    for one year
and that after that year had elapsed
– which it did several months ago –
I would come back and take over.
He consented to this and swore to the gods
    bindingly.
But now he is breaking the agreement –'

Eteocles	(*mocking*) 'The agreement.'
Polynices	Yes you are you liar don't you dare take that tone with me!
Jocasta	Please.

Polynices	'– is breaking the agreement
	not only stealing my share of our father's
	    property
	but addicted – like the worst kind of criminal
	    dictator –
	to total power. Despite that –'

Eteocles	(*mutters*) Criminal dictator / bullshit.

Polynices	'DESPITE THAT' – just listen –
	'despite that even now I would still be
	    prepared –
	provided my brother sees reason –
	(a) to call off the army (b) to refrain from
	further destruction of crops or human
	habitation (c) to refrain from an attempt to
	scale the walls and (d) to restore and
	    maintain
	our original voluntary agreement.
	But – if he continues to treat me unjustly
	when my cause is indisputably just –
	then I have no choice' –
	and our mother completely accepts this –
	'no choice but to wage a just war.
	Forgive me: I cannot make speeches
	but I can state the facts
	and the facts here speak for themselves.'

Girl	Says Polynices.
Polynices	Says – yes – Polynices.

Trembling, he puts away his paper.

Eteocles	(*with contempt*) 'Says Polynices, says
	Polynices.'

(with contempt) 'Says Polynices, says
　　Polynices.'
Listen – *Mummy* – what the fuck is this?
If so-called moral goodness can speak for
　　itself
why have we never heard it? Mmm?
Or is 'Says Polynices' here its sole
　　representative on earth?
What's wrong with total power?
Of course it's a drug:
but it's a drug that turns a human being –
look at me – *I said look at me like Mummy
　　told you to* –
into a god.
I had the balls to take that power –
says the man-king-god-brother-son Eteocles –
and I have the balls now to keep it.
Power means control and control
means security for my – yes they are – my
　　citizens *plus*
don't you come here with your slavering army
of heroic rapists then lecture me
about justice and voluntary agreements.
Who 've you promised first go at your baby
　　sisters? Mmm?
Or given the family history – *Mummy* –
maybe he's saving his sisters
or maybe – who knows? – a more mature
　　lady –
for himself.

Polynices makes a moves towards Eteocles.

You see: he talks about 'seeing reason'
but his own default setting is maximum
　　violence.
Back off – hypocrite. Your plan is to destroy
　　the state.

	Meaning that however much I'm in the wrong
	I'm in the wrong – smiles Eteocles – for the right reasons.
	What d'you think, girls? Good speech?
Girl	We loved it!
Girl	We loved it! – Amazing!
Jocasta	Getting older has some advantages, Eteocles.
	One is to see things in perspective – another
	is to be able to ignore – thank you – gratuitous insults.
	You talk about the state – control – stability – yes? –
	but all I can hear is my own ambitious little boy
	trying to justify grabbing at table the ripest fruit.
	It could almost be – what's the word? – lovable? –
	to observe how this angry young son of mine
	makes the same face he did as an angry baby –
	were it not for the degradation of human society
	that total power facilitates.
Girl	Hangings in stadiums.
Girl	Industrialised killings.
Jocasta	Let me speak.
	Be just, Eteocles – be equitable – listen – reciprocate –
	isn't that the basis of human friendship
	and of lasting human alliances?
Girl	Yes but why should – (*anyone have to listen if they're more powerful?*)

Jocasta   (*cutting her off*) I said let me speak!
Shouldn't we each of us balance our own
     desires
against the desires of others?
Why did we invent the weighing-scales?
Was it simply for the rich to calculate how
     rich they are?
Or was it to make sure that each of our
     citizens
at harvest-time has an equal share of the
     harvest?
The god Night follows the god Day
and without night – Eteocles –
how would we ever sleep?
When would I – for example – ever stop
     hearing
your father's voice screaming and screaming
     inside my head
like it's doing right now – *right now* – hear it?
And if Day's prepared to leave its heat in our
     stone walls
and welcome the Night by turning the sky
     indigo
why can't you – Eteocles – welcome your
     own brother?
Are you suggesting you're more important
     than the sun?
(*Faint laugh.*) D'you think he really believes
     that, girls?
Come on – we're curious – is it the city you
     want to protect
or is it your own authority? Yes yes yes
of course you're going to tell me it's the
     same thing –
but what if you fight now and Polynices wins?
You know what will happen.

34

Destruction of property. Torture. Looting.
Murder. Dismemberment. Blinding. Rape.
Is that what you mean by security?

As for you, Polynices –
oh and don't pretend that won't happen –
can't you see how reckless you've been
to lock yourself by marrying some child
into a permanent alliance?
Because either you win and destroy in the
name of justice
everything you claim here in front of us
to love *or*
you lose and present your new allies
with a butcher's bill for potentially
thousands dead.
And how will they feel about *that*?

Both of you – please – make peace.
I've told you about the screaming in my head:
don't add to it.

Eteocles   Bravo. Marvellous. Let's all lie back shall we
in a nice warm bath of political theory.
Because not one word – *Mummy* – alters
the facts:
the fact I am king, the fact I have power *now*.
That is the situation. It's not negotiable.
You're wasting my time. Leave or I'll have
you killed.

Polynices   'Have me killed'? Oh?

Eteocles   It would be one very practical solution.

Jocasta   Please stop.

Polynices   How? You think I won't take you with me?

Eteocles   Try it.

35

Jocasta	Both of / you stop!
Polynices	Look at him backing away.
Eteocles	Just you try it.
	Pause.
Polynices	I am giving you one last opportunity Eteocles – in front of witnesses – are you listening? – to restore our original agreement.
Eteocles	To divide our father's property.
Polynices	Yes.
Eteocles	To share the executive power.
Polynices	Yes.
Eteocles	As night follows day?
	Pause.
	You're a dangerous child, Polynices. The state's not a bar of chocolate. Break it into two pieces and you will have civil war. Now get out.
Polynices	I won't leave till I've talked to my father.
Eteocles	Not possible.
Polynices	Then I want to talk to my sisters.
Eteocles	(*to Jocasta*) Should we let him talk to his sisters? No. I don't think so.
Polynices	Why not? Let me see them.
Jocasta	I don't think you should, Polynices. It wouldn't / be helpful.

Eteocles	We don't think you should. We've noted your violence / towards women.
Polynices	Helpful? What is she *talking about*?
	Pause.
	(*Softly.*) Where will you be positioned?
Eteocles	I'm sorry?
Polynices	In battle. Where will you be positioned?
Eteocles	Positioned? Wherever. Gate A or wherever. Why?
Polynices	I'll be there. I'll kill you.
Eteocles	Likewise. My pleasure. I trust you can see how much this conversation is upsetting your mother.
Girl	Don't call her upset – she's angry.
Eteocles	(*genial*) And what the fuck's that to do with you, sweetheart? Angry – upset – whatever.
Jocasta	I don't feel anything.
Eteocles	You see: in fact she doesn't feel anything. Come on. We're going. I said Mummy – come on – we're going.
Jocasta	Goodbye, Polynices.
	Jocasta and Eteocles go out, leaving *Polynices and the Girls. He gets his piece of* *paper back out of his pocket and unfolds it.*
Polynices	(*reads*) 'I am calling to witness this land that nurtured me and the gods that I am being driven out of my own city like a slave

and that if anything happens to it now
blame my brother. I refuse to be held
   responsible.'

*Pause. The Girls are getting bored and drift
away.*

'Farewell then to this house
and to you my mother and sisters
who I see listening to me speak with tears
   in your eyes:
farewell. Not that I don't intend to kill
   the man
you see standing so arrogantly here before you
and return to reclaim what is rightfully mine.
These gold stone walls with their seven gates.
These shady courtyard gardens.
Meadows, green tree-tops, our sacred stream.
This Kadmean city of Thebes.'

*No one's listening. He carefully folds up the
sheet of paper. He's completely alone.*

SCENE SIX
GIRLS

——

This was Paradise –
it says here the Phoenician girls sang –
and god (see footnote)
said in his god-voice 'Kadmos –
Kadmos settle here
where the sacred stream
seen in Figure 6
will provide irrigation
for field after field of wheat *plus*
my own son Dionysus
was born here –

38

punched out with his tiny fists
screamed with joy
as green leaves
spiralled around his cot.'

—— Oh sweet!

—— So even today – the author writes here in
   the book –
Theban women are sexually aroused
by loud amplified music.

—— Guarding this weed-lined aquifer in Paradise
for the god of Earth-stroke-War –

—— Sang the Phoenician girls –

—— – sang – yes – the Phoenician girls –
a primitive life-form –

—— – dragon – snake –

—— – a reptile – that's right – kept watch.
Kadmos – who needed water
to wash the sweet sex-smell from his fingers –
pulped its head with a rock
broke out its teeth
and following Athena's instructions
sowed them in the fields shown
on the diagram.
The rest will be familiar to some of you
from cinema: soldiers
break through earth's crust
grow fully armed towards the light
and start killing each other.
The few who survive found Thebes.

—— Look carefully at the map.

—— Yes look carefully at the map.
Where is the supermarket car park?
Can you locate the bus station?

——   Using a soft pencil
            mark where the god of Earth-stroke-War
            blows off the front
            of a concrete apartment block.

SCENE SEVEN

Eteocles paces up and down.

Eteocles   I asked for him to be here now.
            We're wasting time: where is he?

Girl   He's interrogating a prisoner.

Eteocles   He's doing what?

Girl   Interrogating a prisoner.

            Kreon appears. Eteocles doesn't see him.

Eteocles   I need to talk to him *now*.
            I have instructions to give.
            Maybe my idiot uncle hasn't actually grasped
            he's not the one in command here.
            (*Sees him and smiles.*) Kreon.

Kreon   (*smiles*) Eteocles. Busy man.

Eteocles   Yes.

Kreon   Good conversation?

Eteocles   I'm sorry?

Kreon   With your brother – good conversation?

Eteocles   No.

Kreon   Not useful?

Eteocles   No. Sorry. But I hear you have some
                intelligence.

Kreon	That's right. We captured a prisoner. We've been . . .
	Notices he has a spot of blood on him and wipes it off.
	Yes – well – he says an operation's imminent: full mobilisation of troops plus simultaneous assault at each of our seven gates.
Eteocles	Then we should counter-attack immediately.
Kreon	You're sure?
Eteocles	That's what I just said. Is that not what I / just said?
Kreon	You mean open the gates? – Actually leave the city?
Girl	Crush them.
Eteocles	Crush them. Pre-emptive strike. Out through the gates. Yes.
Kreon	And the numbers?
Eteocles	What?
Kreon	We'd be outnumbered, Eteocles, and totally exposed.
Eteocles	The men here are frustrated.
Kreon	I see that.
Eteocles	They need to get out there and fight.
Kreon	Yes I can see that. (*Smiles at Eteocles.*)
Eteocles	We've been through the other options.
Kreon	Of course you have.

Eteocles	(*points at Girl*) Night raid?
Girl	Too much risk – potential chaotic retreat.
Eteocles	(*points at another Girl*) Dawn raid? Dawn raid? – come on.
Girl	Uncertainty of outcome –
Girl	Uncertainty of outcome *plus* risk will create self-defeating diversion.
Eteocles	Good. (*Points at another.*) Cavalry attack?
Girl	Horses would be disembowelled by steel blades of enemy chariot defences.
Girl	That is disgusting.
Eteocles	So what is it you're suggesting, Uncle Kreon: we all stay cooped up here and offer them our unconditional surrender? Well?
	He looks round at Girls. Several raise their *hands. He points at one.*
Girl	Defeatism is a capital offence.
Eteocles	Exactly.
Kreon	Oh?
	Pause.
	Look: according to our intelligence they're planning as I have said – says Kreon an attack at each gate simultaneously with seven separate battalions of approximately nine hundred men. That's over six thousand soldiers. What I'm therefore suggesting to you is stay inside the walls – yes – and assign to each Gate A thru G

	a commander of your own
	to lead a highly aggressive counter-force.

Pause.

Eteocles	Whatever.
Kreon	Speed up the decision-making cycle by a system of clear delegation and brief those / officers now.
Eteocles	Yes yes yes whatever – okay – I'll do it – don't lecture me – don't think I need you to make my decisions for me because I am going to *personally kill him*.

Pause. Kreon smiles.

What?

Kreon	You said you had instructions for me.
Eteocles	Yes. Did I? What instructions?
Girl	If I should die.
Eteocles	Yes if I should die – that's right – thank you – because of my father's sick mind and the way it has infected me and my brother I want you to take responsibility for Antigone and make sure that whatever happens her marriage to your eldest son still goes ahead – do you agree? What's next?
Girl	Teiresias.
Eteocles	Yes and get your other little boy to go and fetch Teiresias. See if you can get out of him some kind of politically useful statement- stroke-prediction –

43

not that it's not mostly bullshit –
but all the same he'll talk to you.

Girl   One last thing.

Eteocles What?

Girl   One last thing.

Eteocles (*softly*) Hmm. Yes. One last thing.
If Polynices for whatever reason dies
you are instructed to forbid burial of the body.
Leave it to rot.
And if anyone attempts burial –
even a family member –
put them to death.
Is that understood?

Pause.

Girl   Says Eteocles.

Eteocles Says Eteocles.

SCENE EIGHT
GIRLS

——   Consider the following list
of steps for preparing an animal sacrifice.

——   1. Garland animal with flowers.

——   2. Plunge torch in water.

——   3. Hide knife under barley inside basket.

——   4. Get hairs from animal and burn.

——   5. When animal nods consent
cut animal's throat ensuring animal's head
is turned to the sky.

44

―――   6. Provide music.

―――   And if / recorded –

―――   Yes if recorded remember to take spare
batteries.

―――   7. Make women repeatedly scream.

―――   8. Catch blood in suitable vessel:
stainless steel is advisable.

―――   9. Flay animal.

―――   10. Burn thighbones for the gods.

―――   11. Pour a little wine on flames.

―――   12. Eat remainder of meat.

―――   On the facing page you will find
instructions for the sacrifice of humans.
Take a few moments to examine the
    photographs
before attempting to answer the questions.
Use at least *three* of the following words
    in your response:

Hero.
Carbon.
Honour.
Cobalt.
Terror.
Freedom.
Earth.
Cadmium.
God.
Power.
Coffee.
Blood.
Family.

Earth.
Destiny.
Make-up.
Race.
Tribe.
Justice.

SCENE NINE

*Teiresias appears at the doorway with his Daughter and
Kreon's son Menoecius.*

Teiresias	Kreon? Kreon? – where are you? Where is he? Talk to me. I said talk to me. I'm not here to play games.
Kreon	You know where I am, Teiresias.

Pause.

Teiresias	What is it you want?
Kreon	It's not me who is / playing games.
Teiresias	What is it – exactly – that you want?

Pause.

Kreon	Our city is under threat.
Teiresias	I know that.
Kreon	The enemy is well / resourced.
Teiresias	I know all about / the enemy.
Kreon	Eteocles –
Teiresias	I don't talk to Eteocles. Eteocles shows / no respect.

46

Kreon	Yes but he's instructed me to ask you what measures we could be taking to protect it.
Teiresias	If any – smiles the prophet.
Kreon	Yes if any.
Teiresias	Kreon. Listen. You've asked me a direct question and that means I'm obliged to answer it.

In a new tone:

The gods warn Laius not to have children
but he does, he has Oedipus and Oedipus
despite taking every possible precaution
kills him and marries his own mother
and when he discovers the hard facts
(a) of patricide and (b) of maternal incest
    he blinds himself
which means tying a knot in human history.

Kreon	We know / all this.

Teiresias	The two sons – oh? – think they can cover
	    this up
	by forcing him out of the public eye:
	they beat him – they spit on his clothes –
	think they can cut through the knot of
	    human history
	but like a cornered animal he howls back
	    at them
	and the knot gets tighter and tighter . . . Yes?

Daughter whispers in his ear.

Those two boys will kill each other, Kreon –
they themselves are the knot –
and their armies will stamp each other's brains
and hacked-off body parts into the meadow

and the whole city will be destroyed
unless you listen to what I have to say
since there is – yes – a solution

He starts to get up.

namely a human sacrifice
for the collective good
but forgive me I'm probably wasting your
    time
with sacred predictions and so on
since the bird-information we've received
about human sacrifice will not necessarily
please you the recipient. – Thank you,
    sweetheart.

Daughter takes his hand to lead him away.

Kreon   Stay where you are.

Teiresias   Don't touch me, Kreon. I'm not one of /
    your slaves.

Kreon   (*to Daughter*) You: let go of him.
I said let go of your father's hand.

Teiresias frees his own hand from her grip.

Tell me what sacrifice you mean.

Teiresias   Kreon. If you're asking me to tell you
then you know that I have no choice.
Where's Menoecius?

Kreon   Menoecius is just over there – why?

Teiresias   I'd like him to leave the room.

Kreon   If these women can be trusted with important
    information
then so can my son.

Teiresias   You want him to listen.

Kreon	Of course. It's in his interest too. It's in everyone's.
Teiresias	Well the solution to saving the city of Thebes according to the bird-information recorded here –

Daughter whispers in his ear.

– is for you, Kreon – to kill him – to kill Menoecius.

Kreon	What 're you talking about?
Teiresias	I told you: a human sacrifice.
Kreon	I don't understand what you mean.

Pause.

NO NOT MY SON.
I take this back. I didn't ask. You didn't speak, you didn't speak, you didn't speak, you didn't speak,
you didn't speak. (*To Girls.*) You heard nothing.
He didn't speak. – No no no this can't be happening.

| Teiresias | You did ask the question and from the political perspective
believe me it is / the solution. |
|---|---|
| Kreon | To hell with the political perspective.
What 're you and this little whore of yours trying to do to me? Eh? |

He grabs Daughter's hair and drags her away from Teiresias.

You fucking poisonous cunt.
What was that shit you were whispering?

Teiresias	The truth, Kreon. Why else would you be hurting her so much?
	Kreon realises this attack is shocking *Menoecius and releases her.*
Kreon	Nobody is to hear about this.
Teiresias	I can't not speak. It would be wrong.
Kreon	So you're happy to go out into the city repeat this in public and sentence my son to death.
Teiresias	I said I must speak. I didn't say happy.
Kreon	Why?
Teiresias	Yes that's always a very good question. Well in this case it's a matter of – remind me, sweetheart, what it's a matter of.

Daughter whispers in his ear.

Oh yes: it's a matter of blood.
You'll remember how Kadmos founded this
    city
by splitting open the dragon's head with
    a rock
where the cool stream the Ismenus ran
with strands of green weed in it?
Well the Earth can't forgive him, Kreon.
The Earth can't forgive *you*
for being the human civilised person you are
since every cell in your human civilised
    body is derived –
don't you feel it? – from that smashed head.
It wants your child.
It wants you to go back to that same stone
    cistern
where Kadmos broke the teeth out of its own
    child's mouth

and – to obtain the city's protection –
   murder your son.
Is that unreasonable?

He gets up.

Children get raped and murdered every day
by men who 're just bored.
This would be an exemplary act
with a clear political objective.
– Thank you, sweetheart.

*Daughter takes his hand again and they
move off.*

I'm so sorry.
I told you I wasn't here to play games.

*They go out. Kreon smashes something.
One of the Girls tries to comfort Menoecius.
He pushes her away.*

Kreon	The collective good? How dare that hypocrite come here hand in hand with his own small precious child and suggest I sacrifice mine? What's wrong?
Boy	I'm frightened – says the small boy – I don't want to stay here. I'm frightened of what he said.
Kreon	I'm sending you away – don't be frightened.
Boy	Away? Where?
Kreon	On a trip. To the temple.
Boy	Oh? – to the temple? – what trip?
Kreon	To the temple at Dodona. The god there will protect you.

Boy	Zeus? But won't I need / money?
Kreon	Yes – will guide and protect you. What did you say?
Boy	Won't I need money? The god will protect me but I'll be frightened alone on a trip without money. What will I eat?
Kreon	Come on – come with me – I'll give you some.
Boy	Please will you get it, Daddy. I'm too frightened. And I need to say goodbye to my Auntie Jocasta because when I was just a tiny tiny baby and poor Mummy was dead she looked after me remember? Please?
	Kreon goes.
	What're you all staring at? Mmm? Maybe where you come from nobody dies for what they believe in because no one believes in anything. Am I right? I'm a man –
Girl	Says the small boy.
Boy	What?
Girl	Says the / small boy.
Boy	No. *Says the man.* I'm a man – *says the man* – and it was right to deceive my father it was right to lie to him for the collective good

and it is right to kill myself now
for the collective good
because I'm a man – don't tell me I'm not.
Bitch. Bitch. Don't stare at me like that.
You think I'm crying?
Well I'm not, bitch – I'm not – I'm angry.
My father is weak and disgusting.
Men here in Thebes grew out of the earth.
They were brave and they killed each other
and the ones who were left
founded this city with blood and constructed
   the walls –
yes they did – yes they did! – with music.
And because I'm a man I will kill myself
   to protect it.

What? What?
What is it you've got? I want to see.
I said don't stare at me like that, bitch
   JUST SHOW ME.

A Girl is holding a butcher's knife with an
ash-wood grip. She seems reluctant to take it
to Menoecius but some of the others push
her forward.

What's that? What's it for?

Girl	(*turning back to the others*) I can't say it.
Girl	Yes you can.
Girl	He's so small.
Girl	Doesn't mean she can't say it. Go on.

Girl with knife overcomes her reluctance and
smiles at Menoecius.

Girl   It's for you.

She offers him the knife. He takes it.

Would you like me to show you how?

Menoecius nods.

Come with me then.

SCENE TEN
GIRLS

—— Listen to the musical extract.

Music: Bach, BWV 127, Aria: 'Die Seele ruht in Jesu Händen'. The plaintive oboe melody cuts through the texture of staccato recorders and pizzicato bass.

In what kind of world was this music written?

—— How many sheep cropped the meadows?

—— How many cars streamed along the motorways?

—— In the green tree-tops of Thebes when this music was written
how many birds precisely nested
and how much data
moved between the machines in offices?

Music continues.

—— When this music was written
who died for which Sphinx?

—— Was that belief a steel needle driven under a fingernail?
Or was it / a comfort?

54

——— Or was the steel needle driven under the
    fingernail
itself the comfort?

——— What is a Sphinx?
What song does a Sphinx sing?

*On music recording, the soprano now enters,
bar 9.*

Is it like this?
Or is it some other song?

The music continues. Everything goes still.

*Then banging at a door. The banging grows
louder. An Officer can be heard shouting
'Hey! Open this door!'*

*The Girls unbolt the door and the Wounded
Officer bursts in. At the same time Jocasta
appears upstairs and watches.*

SCENE ELEVEN
WOUNDED OFFICER

Officer   What's going on? Get me Jocasta!
I need to talk to her.
I said come on – it's important.
What's going on in here?
Get me a drink of water, sweetheart.
What's wrong? Never seen a man bleed?

A Girl gets him water.

Where the hell is she? Crying?

Jocasta   I was taking food to my husband.
I don't have the time to cry.
Well?

If you've come to tell me he's dead, get on
with it.

Officer   Your son is alive. I stood next to him.

Jocasta   Then why are you smiling?
They broke through the gates?

Officer   No one broke through.

Jocasta   But we were attacked?

Officer   What?

Jocasta   I said: but we were attacked?

Officer   Oh yes. But we routed them.

Jocasta   Then why are you smiling at me like that?
Is it Polynices?

Officer   Who?

Jocasta   My son – my son Polynices. What's
happened?

Officer   Polynices is alive. Nothing's happened.

Jocasta   Then why are you smiling? (*Slaps his face.*)
Stop smiling at me like that. (*Slaps his face.*)
Tell me what's happened. (*Slaps his face.*)

Officer   I have excellent news –

*The Officer faints from blood-loss. Some
Girls catch him and lay him down.*

Girl   I have excellent news.
I have excellent news. Say it.
I said *say it.*

Jocasta   I have excellent news.

Girl   Good. Since after that / young man –

| Jocasta | Since after that young man your nephew – |
| | yes – |

| Girl | So intelligently. |

Jocasta	– so intelligently slit his own throat
	we felt really fired up by his sacrifice:
	yes I'll be honest it was like having sex
	only sharper and sweeter –
	forgive me for saying that, says the Officer –
	much sharper much sweeter than fucking
	a girl *plus*
	your son Eteocles is a great great soldier
	and I'm not just saying that:
	he gets you within his mind
	so you're actually within your commander's
	mind
	meaning each of us knew precisely what to do
	at each of Gates A thru G.
	We saw the enemy
	exactly as we expected from our intelligence
	head south-west out of Teumessos
	split off after crossing the river
	ring the whole city
	then take up positions behind their defensive
	earthworks
	carrying white metal shields.
	Attacking Gate A – says the Officer – was
	the Pretty One
	your daughter noticed earlier
	with that picture on his shield
	of his mother
	plus at Gate B the old prophet Amphiaros
	whose shield is blank.
	There was Hippómedon of course –
	says the blood-stained Officer to Jocasta –
	attacking Gate C

	whose shield has multiple steel eyes on it – weird – which snap open or shut according to the light and of course Tydéus – Tydéus, says the Officer, with the device on his shield of Prometheus carrying fire at D oh and at E –
Girl	– he goes on –
Jocasta	– yes at E –
Girl	– he goes on –
Jocasta	– yes attacking Gate E, the Officer goes on, was your son Polynices whose shield as you will be aware shows carnivorous toy horses designed to look insane plus troops at F led by Kapanéus whose fantasy's to lever this whole city of ours out of the earth like a dead tree-stump oh and I mustn't forget says the dying blood-stained Officer to Jocasta no mustn't forget Adrastos your son's new father-in-law by marriage at Gate G whose idea of justice is take every new-born baby he can find and whip its head against a stone wall.
	Pause.
Girl	So we started to fight.
Jocasta	What?
Girl	So we started to fight.
Jocasta	So we started – yes – says the Officer – to fight.

We threw down javelins
into the open mouths of their vanguard.
We used accurate sling-shot
to crack open their pelvic bones.
We had every advantage but that's when
    Tydéus
and your son I mean the enemy son
do I call him that? says the dying
blood-stained Officer to Jocasta
shrieked: WAKE UP. ADVANCE.
GO FOR THE GATES. BURN THE GATES.

Girl   BURN THEM ALIVE. KILL.

Jocasta   Kill. Yes. Yes. So they surged out en masse
from their dugouts
exactly as we expected from our intelligence
and began picking us off quite effectively
with spears and pieces of rock
yes we were taking casualties plus now
    the Pretty One
made a mad run at the Gate: Gate A
so what I did says the Officer was I dropped
says the Officer this sand-stone block
directly on to him so his head popped open
along the sutures of the skull like fruit
his soft skin and his long gold hair crushed
    into it
meaning we could move on from A
says the Officer to the other gates
and Eteocles whose mind I was well inside
    now
yes well well inside my commander's
    excellent mind
was able to rally the men who were wavering
and force them back into the line of fire.
That's when an incident occurred

since Kapanéus who'd calculated
the exact length of ladder
that would extend from ground level
to the top of our city walls
using trigonometry
dragged this ladder into position and started
    to climb it
hunched under his shield and boasting
that not even the holy fire of Zeus
could stop him destroying us
and just as he came level with the coping
    stones
Zeus burned him to death.
Yes – says the blood-stained Officer to
    Jocasta –
Zeus burned him to death – he spun off that
    ladder
with his arms and legs thrown out blazing
    like x
for the unknown quantity in one of his own
    equations
and crashed to the ground and when
    Adrastos saw
that even Zeus was hostile
and could smell the dead man's hair
and the dead man's body-fat actually burning
he pulled back his Greeks to the ring of
    ditches
and that was our cue: we charged out after
    them.

We cut off their feet and hands.
We tore their lungs out.
Their dead lay in heaps.
We leaned over the dying.
We removed their armour.
We sucked out their eyes.

Girl	Victory is good.
Jocasta	Victory is good. Yes.

Pause.

But look – says the dying Officer –
maybe I'm smiling because I'm afraid
of what I'm going to say to you next
because what I'm going to say to you next
says the Officer to Jocasta
is that despite this your sons have now
   decided
to fight to the death in single combat.
Yes – he says – your sons have no shame –
no self-control – I hate telling you this –
hate telling you how Eteocles climbed a
   tower
and called for silence next to the vermilion
   flag –
hate telling you how he grinned and shouted:
   'Peace!' –
how he shouted out: 'No more killing!' –
how he shouted: 'Polynices. Where are you?
If you're a man, step forward.
If you're a man, fight me in single combat now
If I kill you, the city's mine. Kill me, and it's
   yours.
Where are you? Step forward. Accept this
   challenge.
End this violence.' – Hate telling you how
   Polynices
stepped out from the ranks and accepted
and how both armies cheered and cheered
as if the preceding massacre had never
   happened –
how their commanding officers
instructed their soldiers to disarm and swore

that whatever the outcome of the fight
it would be – oh yes – politically binding.
They're putting on armour now.
They're preparing to kill each other right now
and their so-called friends who even now
might be able to stop them
go up to them publicly instead
kiss their mouths
and use words like hero
says the Officer to their
mother

Girls Hero. Carbon.

words like fame – god –
   glory –
city – earth – blood –
hero – honour –
while the religious
   leaders of each side
take care to keep their
   trim beards
well clear of the
   sacrificial spitting
lamb-fat. Antigone!

Honour. Cobalt.
Terror. Freedom.
Earth. Cadmium.
God. Power.
Coffee. Blood.
Family. Earth.
Destiny. Make-up.
Race. Tribe.
Justice.

Pause.

Where is Antigone?
I said: where is Antigone?

Girl   Your daughter's dancing.

Girl   No, she's washing / her hair.

Jocasta   Dancing? Antigone – out here now!
I need you please.
How can she be dancing?
I don't understand. What's justice? What's
   coffee?
What's happening to my mind?

62

Antigone	Mummy? Stop talking to yourself. It's frightening. Who's that man?
Jocasta	Why are you dancing?
Antigone	I'm not. I was washing my hair.
Girl	You see: I was / right.
Jocasta	Shut up.
Antigone	What's wrong? You look mad. Be normal. Please?
Jocasta	Come on: we're leaving. You're going to stop them.
Antigone	I'm not even dressed. Stop who?
Jocasta	Your brothers are trying to kill each other. You're going out there to stop them.
Antigone	I'm not going out there – it stinks – it's horrid – it's all men.
Jocasta	It's always all men. Deal with it.
Antigone	What can I do?
Officer	You can plead, sweetheart.
Jocasta	You can plead. Go down on your knees. Tell them that killing each other means killing me.

—— Why is the man in the check shirt wearing a green hat?

—— The middle-aged man lying next to the bucket is partially clothed. Discuss the role of clothing in human sacrifice and for an extra point explain the significance of the bucket.

—— Why is the black pit filled with pink flowers?

—— Are you jealous of Silvana Mangano's dress?

—— My name is Steffi: true or false?

—— In Figure 3 a whole family has been sacrificed including the mother. Does this make the sacrifice more likely to fail or to succeed? Give reasons for your answer.

—— Are you jealous of Silvana Mangano's eyes?

—— Yes why pink? And what has the sacrifice achieved?

—— What's my name? Is it Miriam?

—— Why do the angles of a triangle add up to 180°?

What is the boiling-point of glass? Give reasons for your answer.

—— Examine the sacrificial pit. How common are pits of this kind nowadays? Who makes them and why? This one is filled with flowers. Why pink?

—— Are you jealous of Silvana Mangano's mouth or hair?

—— How
does it feel when
I climb your
body?

—— How
does it feel when
I climb your
body? What can
you see through
the mineral ring
of my iris?

—— Can you
see the mica
flakes that make
up the mineral
ring of my iris?

—— Is god
also a triangle?
Give reasons for
your answer.

SCENE THIRTEEN

Kreon enters, subdued.

Kreon   Where's my sister?
I said to you where is my sister?

A Girl goes up to him and tenderly touches his shoulder.

Girl   What's happened?

Kreon   Why did you let him go?

Girl   Let who go?

Kreon   My son.

In spite of himself, he leans into a Girl for comfort, making a strange cry of grief.

Girl   He died for his city, Kreon.
He needed to make that sacrifice.

Girl   It's not your fault.
You tried to stop him: you couldn't.

Kreon speaks inaudibly.

We can't hear what you're saying.

Kreon   (*tearful*) Where did he get the knife?

He breaks away from Girl.

Girl   Look, why don't you come and sit down –
you're in shock.

Girl   If somebody's determined to do something,
Kreon,
they find a way.
If somebody wants a knife they find one.

Kreon   I know. Forgive me.

Girl   Come on.

Kreon   Forgive me.

*He allows Girl to take his hand and lead him
to a chair.*

I've carried him back to my house.
He's laid out on the floor
– but there's blood.
Yes there's still blood
and my poor poor boy needs to be washed.
Properly washed. Cleansed.
Because I'm a human civilised person
and human civilised people care for the dead.
Where's my sister? He needs his family.
He needs to be properly washed.

Girl   Jocasta's not here, Kreon.
She left with Antigone.

Kreon   What d'you mean, left? Why?

Girl   Well she was told that her two boys –

Girl	Yes that her two boys were intending to fight in single combat to settle the what? – the –
Girl	The political question.
Girl	– that's right – the political question. So she went out to try and stop them.

Unnoticed by Kreon, a Softly-Spoken Officer appears.

Kreon	When? Why wasn't I told?
Girl	It was hours ago. It must be all over.
Kreon	How can it be hours ago? Time hasn't passed. What're you girls / *talking about?*
Officer	Your sister is dead, Kreon. She killed herself. I'm sorry.
Kreon	Time hasn't passed. What do you mean?

Pause.

Officer	The two boys killed each other and Jocasta then killed herself.
Girl	Of course time has passed. You're in shock. Why don't you just –
Kreon	Don't touch me!

Pause.

Officer	Yes I'm afraid the fight took place immediately. They found a level patch reasonably clear of stones and so on: I'd say it was about thirty by thirty metres –
Girl	Nine hundred metres squared.

Officer	Thereabouts – thank you – and Polynices –
Girl	About the size of two tennis-courts.
Officer	Okay – thank you – and Polynices read out a kind of prayer to Hera her being the goddess of marriage and so on asking her help to kill his brother saying he'd drag the mutilated body back to his bride – who's just a little girl, I think –
Girl	Argeia. She's eleven.

Officer	Eleven years old – exactly. Which raised
	   eyebrows
	even among his own supporters.
	And – um – Eteocles –
	yes Eteocles also prayed if that's the correct
	   word
	to Zeus's daughter –

Girl	Pallas Athena.
Officer	– yes to Pallas Athena: 'Oh give me strength in my right arm to thrust this spear deep into my brother's heart.' Something like that plus he also raised a number of points about real politics versus political theory only it was pretty hot out there in the sun and no one was listening particularly. D'you think I could have a drink?

One of the Girls gets water.

Anyway – thank you – the signal to start
was a trumpet –
one long high note like a beam of light –

68

and they were fighting before it'd even ended.
I won't call them animals –
they were just boys –
but all the same it's hard to describe what
    happened
without thinking about animals –
or maybe two insects trapped in a jar.
They'd crouched down behind their shields
    you see
and if either glimpsed the other one's head
    peep over
they jabbed at it with a spear
and struck sparks off the metal.
This little game of reflex stabbing
went on silently for some time till Eteocles –
says the softly-spoken Officer –
stumbled over a stone.
He kicked it to one side with his foot
but in so doing exposed his left calf-muscle
which Polynices' spear-point immediately slit.
His whole army cheered
but Polynices had actually lost concentration
since Eteocles was able to strike back hard
at his brother's exposed chest
where the tip of his own spear cut here into
    the breast-bone
and snapped off.
Effectively spear-less Eteocles
reached back for a slab of rock
pitched it towards the other boy's spear and
    smashed it.
Can you hear what I'm saying?

Girl   Yes of course.

Officer   Just I tend to speak rather softly
              says the softly-spoken Officer.

69

Girl	We can hear you.
Officer	I've damaged my voice.
Girl	It's okay.
Officer	Good.

Officer
Good.
Well the two boys had no choice now
    basically
but to draw swords and come in close.
They screamed. They battered each other
with their shields. They hacked at each
    other's armour.
Then Eteocles did this move he'd picked up
    in Thessaly –
I don't know if you've come across it? –
where he flipped his whole weight through
    a hundred and eighty degrees
so he was suddenly leading with his right foot
at the same time driving the full length of
    his sword
deep into his brother's lower abdomen.

Polynices jackknifed and collapsed
and Eteocles assumed it was over.

He dropped his sword, knelt down,
and began stripping his brother's body.
And please don't think I'm criticising –
I know that is the military convention
we all of us here follow –
but my point is that Eteocles as commander
made a serious error of judgement.
Since Polynices – who was actually still
    breathing –
had kept hold of his sword and now stabbed it
expertly into Eteocles' liver
knowing he'd bleed to death.
Thus to sum up –

says the softly-spoken Officer to the
    assembled company –
neither has clarified the political situation
but each has a mouth crammed with blood
    and dirt.

Pause.

It was at this point two women
ran up to them.
One was their mother
the other their sister Antigone.
Yes I can see what their mother was doing
    there
but it was obscene to 've dragged along
    that child.
The moment she got close
she started to throw up.
Sick down her top
plus hundreds of men staring.
I don't think the mother noticed:
she went down on her hands and knees
and crawled over her mutilated boys
like a dog picking through rubbish.
She punched Eteocles' face and slapped it
and slapped it till the girl grabbed her arm
and shouted out 'Mummy. Stop.'
She stopped immediately.
She stood up and smiled.
She hooked her daughter's hair
back behind her ears and must've said
    something like
'I'm coming. Wait for me over there,' since
    the girl nodded
and started to walk away.
That's when Jocasta turned back
to her two dead boys and cut her own throat.

	Well each side got up fast and began shouting.

Well each side got up fast and began shouting.
We claimed Eteocles had won –
they said Polynices, seeing he'd drawn first
    blood.
Some people said no one.
It was chaos.
In the absence of clear leadership
I'm afraid we had no alternative:
we'd stayed close to our weapons – they
    hadn't.
They started to run. We slaughtered them.

Kreon   I want him out of this house.

Officer   I'm sorry?

Kreon   Oedipus. I want him out of this house *now*.
He made this happen.
If he hadn't married my sister
she'd still be alive.
My son would still be alive.

Girls react.

What? – What?

Girl   Tell him.

Girl   But you're the one promised her
to whoever could answer the Sphinx's question.

Girl   The answer's a human being – remember?

Kreon bows his head.

Officer   We took casualties – obviously.
There's a small butcher's bill to take care of.

Girl   Plus the girl.

Officer   Yes. Plus the girl.

Antigone   What girl?
Is he talking about me?
What's wrong?
What're you staring at, softly-spoken Officer?
Is it my clothes? Do I smell?
Or is it my hair?
'You wait over there,' she said.
'I'm coming,' she said.
'I won't be a moment,' she said. 'Be brave.'
Be brave be brave be brave:
I'm being brave *what is the fucking use*
oh and what do you think of my hair –
    Mummy –
when I do *this* with it?

*She grips her hair with two hands at first in
a 'pose' but then with growing intensity as if
she would tear it out:*

Thebes is a city
located between two rivers.
To what does it owe
its outstanding economic importance?
Is it (a) to investment in new technologies
(b) to the cultivation of olives
or (c) to copper and tin
or (d) to copper and tin
or (e) to copper and tin
or (f) to copper and tin
or (g) to copper and tin . . .

*She continues to move through the alphabet
repeating these words now almost inaudibly.*

73

Kreon	Get him down here.
Officer	I'm sorry? Get who?
Kreon	Her father. Upstairs. Get him to make her stop.

Officer runs up the stairs, unlocks the door, and goes in. A moment passes – he reappears with Oedipus and forces him too quickly down the stairs, so he stumbles and slides. Antigone's chanting of 'copper and tin' goes on. Officer positions Oedipus near Antigone. Oedipus touches her and says her name. She immediately starts slapping and punching him:

Antigone TICK ONE BOX ONLY!
DO NOT CROSS OUT!
WRITE YOUR NAME!
AT THE TOP OF EACH PAGE!

*She punches and punches before allowing her father to hold her. A moment of stillness.
A radio can be heard playing very faintly in Oedipus' room.*

Oedipus (*gently*) Well. Sweetheart. That hurt.
Tell me something: d'you love me?

Antigone mumbles.

Speak up.

Antigone Yes.

Oedipus And what's wrong?

Antigone I can't say it.

Oedipus Why not?
Can I please say something to you?

Antigone	What? I don't know.
Oedipus	Don't cry. You are never to cry. Promise? Now tell me what's happened.
Antigone	You know what's happened.
Oedipus	It's my boys – your brothers.
Antigone	Yes.
Oedipus	They're dead.
Antigone	Yes.
Oedipus	Then say it. Come on. Don't be afraid.
Antigone	My brothers are both dead.
	Pause.
Oedipus	(*smiles*) Was that so painful?
Antigone	No – yes – yes – yes – no – I don't know.
Oedipus	Where's your sister?
Antigone	I don't know. Why? She's got music.
Oedipus	Where has she got music?
Antigone	I don't know. In the house.
Oedipus	Where in the house? Is that her – or is it my radio?
Antigone	I don't know. Stop asking me questions!
Oedipus	What's wrong with asking you questions?
Antigone	Everything – stop – it's just music.
Oedipus	Frightened I'll make you smile?
Antigone	You won't make me smile. I told you to stop!
Oedipus	Are you sure I won't make you smile?

Slight pause. Faint smile from Antigone.

Why did they let me out? Who else is here?

Antigone No one.

Oedipus Tell me the truth.

Antigone No one. Kreon. And an officer.

Oedipus (*smiles*) Kreon. Why? Where's our mother?

Antigone I can't.

Oedipus Can't what?

Antigone Don't call her *our mother*.

Oedipus Why not? Where is she?

Antigone I can't.

Oedipus She shouldn't've taken you out there.

Officer I told them that.

Pause.

Oedipus Our mother's dead too.

Antigone Yes.

In grief, Oedipus turns his head away,

What?

Oedipus Kiss me.

Antigone No.

Oedipus Won't you kiss me?

Antigone No. Sorry. I can't.

*Pause.**

* In the original production Oedipus was kissed here by one of the Sphinx-girls and a cut was taken in the text to the point marked with a † on page 83.

76

Oedipus	(*smiles*) Kreon.
Kreon	What?
Oedipus	My daughter smells. Can someone please provide her with a change of clothes. Come on, sweetheart – take these off.
Kreon	Apart from the inappropriateness – Oedipus – of asking your own daughter to publicly undress – please do not remove your clothes! – I think you need to understand –
Oedipus	Oh?

Kreon	– Yes – yes – who is in charge here.
	Your daughter is about to marry my
	    surviving son –
	Eteocles gave that explicit instruction –
	and the consequence is: authority rests
	    with me.
	Is that quite clear? Good. Plus –
	Oedipus – I'm sorry but I want you out.
	It's not personal. We all know you've suffered.
	But politically you're a virus
	and you infect everything. Understood?

Oedipus	(*smiles*) Kreon. Congratulations on your
	    new appointment.
	I'm delighted for you.
	But are you quite sure you can't find
	room for me on your team?
	You see, I'm an expert in unhappiness.
	Send me your citizens and for a fee
	I will conduct workshops in how not to live.
	You think you can take even one step now
	across this floor without slipping? Mmm?
	    Try it.

Because there's a film of blood right here.
Right here
under your feet. You don't see it. You're
  blind.
But I can. I see it. And I know it will spread
  out
from this city till it stains like a petrochemical
  disaster
even the most sacred stream.

Come on, Kreon! Lighten up! I'm joking!
Let's celebrate!
Let's go round the back of the bus station eh?
and find us a couple of nice clean flute-girls –
just you and me – what d'you say? –

Antigone   Please stop it.

Oedipus   – get them to slide their fingers
right up our marvellous arses but I'll tell
  you something Kreon
when you push that needle into your eye
it's nothing – strange – just like you're riding
  your bike
and get hit by a piece of grit.
It's only afterwards the light starts dimming.

With new intensity:

Both of my sons.
You're quite sure it's both of them?
And my mother as well. Why her?
Don't make me leave the house.
Kreon? This is all I have.
I'm still young. You need me. I can help you.

Kreon   (*gently*) I'm sorry. It isn't possible.
I'd like you to pack your things.

Antigone   You've no right to just / throw him out!

Oedipus   (*softly*) Antigone – don't.

Kreon   He's not the only person I hope you realise
whose children have died today.
(*To Officer.*) Now listen. Logistics.
    I want Eteocles
properly washed. I want Polynices' body
removed from that bag and dumped.
Before that, make an announcement:
anyone found trying to bury it
will be put to death. Antigone:
you will go back now to your room please
and stay there. I'm not angry. You're a child.
And your father's right:
you should never 've been subjected to this.
    I'm sorry.

Antigone   Don't call me a child.

Kreon   (*to Officer*) And when I say dumped I mean it.
You will forget he's part of our family: that
    body / is toxic.

Antigone   Don't call me a child.
What gives you the right to do this to my
    father?
How's he supposed to live?

Kreon   Listen sweetheart – just go back / to your
    room.

Antigone   How's he supposed to live?
And what d'you mean, toxic? Who says?

Kreon   The decision is out of my hands.

Antigone   Who says? I hate you.
Don't just stand there smiling.

Kreon   The decision is out of my hands.
And you're wrong if you think / I'm smiling.

Girl	He means Eteocles.
Antigone	What?
Girl	The decision. He means / Eteocles.
Kreon	The instruction – she's right – yes – came from your brother Eteocles. Now keep away.
Antigone	But the instruction is wrong. It's wrong. (*To Oedipus.*) Why aren't you saying anything? Tell him the instruction is wrong. This isn't human.
Kreon	Don't you tell me young lady what is or is not human. You will keep away from the body.
Antigone	Why?
Kreon	Somebody tell her. Yes? Yes? You.
Girl	Polynices is an enemy / of the state.
Kreon	Is an enemy of the state. Thank you.
Antigone	What 'state'? This is his home.
	Pause.
	Then I'll bury him myself.
	To Oedipus, who is distracted by hearing the Girls speak.
	Why don't you say something? Help me.
Oedipus	What?
Antigone	Help me.
Oedipus	I can't.

Antigone	You're my father.
Oedipus	He'll kill you.
Antigone	So?

Pause.

At least let me clean him. Get me some water. (*To Officer.*) You. Water. (*He doesn't move.*) (*To Girls.*) One of you then. DO IT!

No one moves.

Then let me kiss him.

Antigone goes and opens the bag – gags – but kisses Polynices' mouth.

Kreon	Very good – that's enough now. You've made your point.

Makes sign to Officer who goes to take hold of her.

You're upsetting your father.
Go to your room.

Antigone	No.
Kreon	I said you will go back to your room.

The Officer has hold of her. She struggles.

Antigone	I don't have to marry. I don't have to give you 'authority'. Let me go.
Kreon	Oh? What's the alternative, sweetheart? Providing sexual services to the military? Tell her, Oedipus.
Antigone	I'll kill him. Then you'd have no sons at all. You'd know what it felt like you cunt.

Kreon signs to Officer, who releases her.

Kreon   You both have one hour to pack.

Kreon leaves with the Softly-Spoken Officer.

Antigone Why won't you defend yourself?
What's wrong with you?
Don't let him talk to us like that.
Stop him.

Kreon has gone.

Oedipus   (*smiles*) Why didn't you say?

Antigone Say what? You've let him go.

Oedipus   You said Kreon and an officer.
You didn't tell me about the others.

Antigone What others?
They're just girls.

Oedipus   Oh?

Antigone Yes.

Oedipus   What girls?

Antigone I don't know. Phoenician girls.
Does it matter?

Oedipus   What d'you mean, Phoenician girls?
Why 're they here?

Antigone They're always here.

Oedipus   Why? What do they want?

Antigone I don't know. Stop asking me questions.
Why did you let him talk to us like that?
What is wrong with you?

Oedipus   (*softly*) Change your clothes now.
Go upstairs and look for my passport.

	See if you can find me a pair of shoelaces.
	Pack the radio: there's money inside it.
	I'm hungry.
	There's a bar of chocolate
	on the floor next to my mattress.
	At the airport we can buy batteries
	and I think I would like a new toothbrush.
Antigone	Toothbrush?
Oedipus	Maybe electric.
Antigone	Toothbrush? How are we going to *live*?
Oedipus	Please. There isn't much time.
	Antigone runs upstairs and off. †
Oedipus	(*to Girls*) I thought I had answered your question.
Girl	Question?
Girl	What question?
Oedipus	What is it I've done?

SCENE FIFTEEN
GIRLS

——	What's this in my fist?
	Is it a stone? Is it a coin?
——	Is it a sacred unspeakable object?
——	Or is it a fist of ash?
——	Yes is it a fistful of ash and bone?
	And when I open my fingers like this
	what do my fingers smell of? Is it sex?
——	Where is the world?

83

—— Good question.

—— What did you do? Select and click?

—— What did you delete?

—— Was it the light? Was it the tree? – stone walls? –
was it the magnificent Theban horses
and comforting sirens of the police?

—— Or was it your own human material? Well?

Pause.

—— What does a Sphinx want plus
who does a Sphinx fuck when?
What does a blind man see
when he looks through the mineral ring of
    her iris?

—— What film do you endlessly project
in the deserted cinema of my mind?

MEN ASLEEP

(SCHLAFENDE MÄNNER)

Men Asleep, in a German translation by Ulrike Syha, as *Schlafende Männer*, was first performed on the MalerSaal stage at Deutsches Schauspielhaus Hamburg, on 17 March 2018. The cast, in alphabetical order, was as follows:

Paul Paul Herwig
Josefine Josefine Israel
Tilman Tilman Strauß
Julia Julia Wieninger

Director Katie Mitchell
Set Design Alex Eales
Costume Design Clarissa Freiberg
Sound Design Donato Wharton
Lighting Design Fabiana Piccioli
Dramaturg Sybille Meier
Voice of Marko Josef Ostendorf

Characters

Julia
Paul
Josefine
Tilman

Paul and Julia are heading for fifty
Josefine is in her twenties, Tilman in his thirties

ONE

Paul, Julia.

Julia Look: what reason was there to have a child?
There was no more reason for you and I to have a child
then, than there is for people to have a child now. No –
there was no reason to have a child, Paul – and – from
my perspective – no desire to. Sure, a child might've
filled a gap in our lives – or – correction – might've been
a channel – a channel of communication between two
people who were estranged before they even met. But if
you think that a child – *that* child, if we're going to be
specific – if you think that *that* child would mean that
we still loved each other, you are wrong, you are wrong,
a child cannot serve that function, Paul, any more than
a screaming baby can.

A child is no guarantee of anything. It doesn't 'ground'
you. It doesn't 'alter the world' in a particularly novel
way – unless it's to make you more selfish. Two people
with a child can hit each other. They can hit the child.
They can hit the child and at the same time persuade the
child to love them. They can do this to each other too.
You could hit me. You could hit me and a moment later
tell me you love me and I would believe you. The
evidence? The punch itself. The slap. But you've never
hit me. You've never tested my love that way. And
besides, since we've stopped loving each other, why
would you test my love? You don't love me, so you don't
hit me. You're calm. You're normal. I like that about

you. You were never any different. Oh you had a little fire once. And so did I. We both had a little more fire. Now we have none. Or next to none. Fire for our work perhaps. Yes, we've gone on being successful in our respective domains – almost surprisingly so – and that is a good thing, surely.

Paul When did I ever hit you?

Julia You've never hit me. I've just said that. And you never will, Paul. You'll never hit me, just like you'll never kiss me. That's perfectly normal. You've lost interest in my mouth. You've lost interest in my eyes. You've lost interest in a lot of the things that interested you when you had more fire. But why would you not? Would it not be odd of you to still be interested? Look. I'm not going to embarrass you. When those two young people come through that door, as they inevitably will, I'm not going to embarrass you. I'm not going to persuade either of those two young people to take an interest in my mouth, my eyes, I'm not going to preen myself in front of them, if that's what you think, I don't plan to solicit sex – why would I solicit sex? – to compensate for my 'loss'? Because the fact is I don't feel that we have a loss, Paul, I feel that we have a bond, and thank God there is no child, no flesh-and-blood actually-existing child that we can exploit now to tear each other apart.

Have you watched couples divorce, Paul? Have you watched how they fill their own children's minds with poison in order to control the outcome of a divorce? But we shan't divorce, Paul. Why should we divorce? Are you asking me, Paul, for a divorce? The idea's ludicrous. We split up and then what? And anyway, why? I don't suffer from my relationship from you. And you're not suffering – are you? – on account of me. Of course not.

Paul Why should I want to leave you?

Julia That's what I mean.

Paul I'm not going to leave you, Julia.

Julia That's what I mean. You're not. You never will.

Pause.

So when those two people – those two young people come through that door –

Paul What people? What door? Why should anybody come and see us? It's two in the morning. No one will visit now. It's two o'clock, Julia. No one has been invited and no one will come. We've cooked nothing. We've prepared nothing. Neither of us drinks. There's no alcohol in the house. There's nowhere to sit – or only these very uncomfortable chairs. What would we talk about? Our jobs? Our domains? No. No one will come and see us. No one will talk to us ever. About anything. Not ever. What is it you imagine? Two people out there in the street? Young man and woman, Julia, out there in the street? With some scrunched-up bit of paper or phone message with our address on it? Heading towards us? Heading towards our building? Really? When did you last write our address on a piece of paper or send it in a message? When did a person last head towards our building at two o'clock in the morning and ring the bell? That's not how we live. How do you think we live? Even when we had what you call fire we didn't live like that. We worked, we ate, we slept, Julia, and we worked again. Even at weekends you went into your department and worked. You worked through bombings. You worked through murder. Not one murder stopped you working – right through the night if necessary. You ate. I ate. Both of us worked and ate. I too went into my department. I too ate. I grew my department. I recruited staff. I branched out into territory that is so far from where I began that even now I find it hard to accept that that is the true locus of my talent. Lost interest in your eyes? Why? Why did you say that? Why do you say that now?

Buzzer. Julia goes over.

Why have you chosen to say that now? Julia?

Julia (*into intercom*) Hello?

Josefine (*voice, brightly*) It's Josefine.

Julia (*into intercom*) Okay. It's open. (*To Paul.*) Why have I chosen to say it now? You think I choose what I say to you? You think there's a range? You think I select what to say to you from a range? A over B or D rather than X? I have no capacity to choose. I have no capacity to select one word over another or any one thought, Paul, over another. You know that about me. (*Knocking.*) you know by the time – IT'S OPEN – know by the time I've said something my mind has moved totally on, moved totally on, Paul, into a new zone in which just like the old zone there is no question of anything like self-consciousness or control.

Josefine and Tilman are standing in the doorway.

Josefine Julia!

Julia Josefine!* Welcome!

TWO

Julia, Paul, Josefine, Tilman.

Josefine We were doing a lot of drugs. We were drinking a lot. We were waking up and it was already evening. We were having great sex but we couldn't remember it.

Paul So how did you –?

* NB this name has four syllables.

Josefine How did we know? Well our friends took photographs. We could see from the photographs it was really great sex but then we'd wake up and it was getting dark and our minds were completely blank!

Paul Oh?

Josefine And of course we could feel in our bodies a kind of deep well-being but the deep well-being was so fucked up by the drugs that you couldn't trust it. We couldn't trust ourselves. We couldn't trust our minds. We couldn't be sure that the feeling of deep well-being was real. We didn't really know what was going on. I'd pull back the blind and it was already dark. I'd kick Tilman and I'd say, 'Tilman, what time is it, it's dark.' But Tilman had no idea. He just lay there smoking and then we'd make love again. I mean that's why I so respect Julia and yourself – you're both so stable – you've been together what? – for years and years – I admire that, it's unusual, my own parents were violent, they were so angry, even with a pillow over my head I could still hear the two of them fighting and screaming.

Pause. Paul is staring at her.

What?

Paul You remind me of Ulrike Meinhof.

Julia Paul?

Josefine I remind you of Ulrike Meinhof?

Paul Don't you think? – don't you think? – something about that smile.

Josefine Ulrike Meinhof killed herself.

Paul (*genial*) Sure – but I'm not talking about that – I'm talking about your smile – it's the smile of someone who still has the whole of her life ahead of her – and if it's any consolation, we don't remember having sex either.

Josefine Consolation – why do I need consolation?

Paul Oh? – I thought for these moments of blankness – am I wrong?

Julia Paul is confused. Paul is confusing an image of Ulrike Meinhof with Ulrike Meinhof. When Ulrike Meinhof died, Paul was a little boy.

Paul She's absolutely right.

Julia Paul knows nothing about Ulrike Meinhof – has only seen images – and even those images he does not have the capacity to understand.

Paul She's absolutely right.

Julia It's not his domain and of course he's normally asleep by now.

Pause.

Josefine Oh – are we not supposed to be here?

Julia Of course you're supposed to be here.

Josefine Because you wrote your address on a piece of paper – Tilman, have you got that piece of paper? –

Julia Of course you're supposed to be here. We invited you.

Josefine Tilman – Tilman – piece of paper.

Paul What's your domain, Tilman?

Tilman My domain? – I can't find it –

Paul Yes your domain – are you Art History too?

Tilman Am I what? – no –

Josefine Tilman – where is the piece of paper?

Tilman I'm looking, I'm looking –

Josefine He's so funny – look at him looking –

Tilman We've talked about having kids, but the kid couldn't be like me, it would have to be like Josefine, it would have to have Josefine's eyes, and Josefine's mouth and hands, and it would have to have her mind and body and Josefine's smile, and Josefine's voice, and Josefine's whole outlook on life because what I am is a piece of shit. I'm not in control. Look at me: I can't even find a piece of paper. I've stopped drinking, I've stopped smoking, I've stopped using drugs and I still can't find it. Because what is this in my pocket, I've no idea, I've never seen it before, I don't even know what is *in my own pockets*, there's something wrong with my mind, and I don't mean in a in a in a dignified way like a true mental illness, I just mean my mind is like shit and if I had a child and the child turned out like me then I'd feel I'd failed, I'd feel I'd failed because the child would fail too and I would just be standing there watching my own child fail like a piece of shit, going through its pockets and failing to find the one thing it had been asked for, and I'd be its father and I would've *made that happen*. And I'd so be so full of love for my failed child, I couldn't bear it.

Pause.

Josefine Tilman makes furniture.

Tilman Yea – yea – Tilman makes furniture.

Josefine To answer your question.

Paul My question?

Josefine About his domain –

Tilman Yea – yea – about my domain.

Josefine He's being funny, because in fact he's very successful –

97

Tilman Yea – yea – very successful.

Josefine He runs a small factory down by the old pumping station. He employs twenty-five people. Tilman is the managing director.

Tilman Tilman is the managing director – yea – yea.

Julia Fantastic!

Tilman Is that your balcony?

Julia Sure.

Tilman D'you mind if I just? –

Julia Please. Go ahead.

Tilman goes out.

Pause.

Josefine What is your domain, Paul?

Paul My domain?

Josefine Yes – what is it?

Julia Can I get you something, Josefine? – glass of water?

Paul How would you describe my domain, sweetheart?

Julia The thing is is that most people of Paul's age who've failed are bitter – but Paul is without bitterness.

Paul I'm without bitterness because I haven't failed. I've built up an enormous department and at the same time people in the industry are queuing to sit at my feet.

Josefine Oh?

Paul Don't say 'Oh', say 'That's really fascinating, Paul'.

Josefine What industry is that?

Julia I'll get you some anyway. (*Goes to get water.*)

Paul Would you like a fight, Josefine?

Josefine What kind of fight? Sure. Why not?

Paul D'you box?

Josefine Not much – but I'd give it a go.

Paul You'd fight a man?

Josefine I'd fight anyone.

Paul And win?

Josefine I think so. Sure.

Julia Bam! Kapow! Blow to the body! Blow to the head!
Split lip. Broken skull. Unconsciousness and death.
Cheers.

She gives Josefine a glass of water.

Josefine Thank you.

They both watch her sip the water.

Julia The water up here's often very warm. We run it
and run it but it stays warm. No one knows why. I think
about it sitting in the pipes waiting to come out. What
d'you think it thinks about while it's waiting?

Paul Let her drink her water in peace.

Julia She's drinking her water in peace. D'you think
people in their homes are more themselves or less? I say
that because Josefine only knows me from her first week
at work, now suddenly she's in my home, and of course
at work I'm a what, I'm an intellectual fury and my
colleagues defer to my encyclopaedic knowledge and
know I can wring political-historical blood out of an
image to the very last drop, but maybe at home I'm a
very different person – am I? am I? – less focused?
maybe much more discursive? what d'you think? Am

99

I still the work-fury, or am I surprisingly relaxed and a natural married hostess who puts everyone at their ease?

Pause. Josefine sips her water.

Of course you don't have to answer me but my perception of *you* has already altered since in just a few minutes I find out you have violent parents and a rich husband – some kind of capitalist! – is that why you sometimes wear such expensive jewellery? – forgive me, forgive me, I was saying to Paul I really don't control my thoughts and the reason for that is I don't believe in free-will, I have no control over what I say or what happens, there are simply electro-chemical things of great complexity and beauty inside of me controlling me, controlling you, controlling Paul – who hates to be told that, look at him, but it's true, Paul – and I am no more in control of my actions than the small animals in that water – is he going to stay out there all night?

Josefine Animals?

Paul She means micro-organisms.

Julia goes over to the balcony door and taps on the glass. Tilman turns.

Julia (*as she goes*) I thought the days of men explaining to women what women mean were over, Paul.

Paul (*intimately, to Josefine*) Not if what the woman is saying is stupid.

Tilman comes back in.

Josefine Dr Haas wants to wrestle with me.

Paul Box – box – and please call me Paul.

Tilman Great view – east-facing? – coldish light – but still: The East. We've got this guy Bobby – checker and packer – used to teach astrophysics – every Friday it's shoes off, down on the mat. I'm into religions – in another life I could've led people – imam – priest – I'd've liked a flock, I'd've liked a community – I mean beyond the community of time-wasting drug-abusers –

Josefine You do lead people, Tilman.

Tilman Yea, yea – 'motivate'. But I mean inside – the thing inside – the spirit – the whatever it's called – the human soul – because excuse me but what is it we're all here for? – is it for dinner or drinks or . . .? I'm getting quite hungry – d'you have anything in your fridge? –

Josefine That is their fridge, Tilman.

Tilman I'm just opening the door. I'm just taking a look. Is that okay?

Julia Sure.

Josefine I think what the water's thinking about is its journey through the human body. It's going to be inside you like a lover is. So it sits there in the pipe waiting and wondering who it's going to penetrate. And of course like everyone it's hoping for a tense young body to fill but knows that it really can't choose and may be simply destined to wash off the piss and the shit.

Slight pause.

Paul Bravo! Bravo, Josefine!

Julia This is why we employed her – for her imagination. But tell me, Josefine, are you saying the water in this apartment is particularly reluctant to flow?

Josefine Not at all.

Julia Because we are the generation of piss and shit?

Josefine Not at all – generation? – no – you asked me what the water was thinking –

Paul You asked her what the water was thinking, sweetheart – she was just trying to –

Julia Just trying to what?

Josefine Just trying to lighten the tone.

Julia Oh? Was the tone not light?

Josefine I mean Tilman and his stupid search for the human spirit – I was just –

Tilman Greek cheese? What's this for?

Paul Ah – ah – for my famous Greek salads.

THREE

Paul, Tilman.

Paul is looking at Tilman's phone

Paul So you read things like 'The Beethoven was of interest but lay firmly in Brendel's shadow' – or 'His Schubert was immaculate but strangely colourless'. And you think, well I've been playing piano since the age of three, should I be angry?

Tilman There's herbs on this cheese, yea?

Paul Oregano.

Tilman That's a Greek thing, is it?

Paul It's a very Greek thing. Should I be angry? How should I react? Nearly twenty years go by in which everyone's been telling you you're a genius – and then . . .

Tilman No one ever told me I was a genius.

Paul But if they did, Tilman – if they did.

Just pick the onions out of that if you don't like them.

Pause. He passes the phone back to Tilman.

So anyway these pictures are . . .?

Tilman Me and Josefine.

Paul I can see it's you and Josefine but what d'you want me to say?

Tilman What d'you *want* to say?

Paul I don't want to say anything.

Tilman Twenty years – Josefine's not much older than that now –

Paul I don't want to say anything.

Tilman Nothing at all?

Paul Why don't you tell me about this furniture of yours.

Tilman Really? Nothing at all?

Paul I want to hear about the furniture.

Tilman The furniture is boring.

Paul I don't believe that.

Tilman The furniture thing is really really boring but okay – sure – if you work in an office you probably sit in one of our chairs. And you probably work at one of our tables. And so successful are our chairs and tables that people are buying them for their homes now – not just to work at – although people are working in their homes, obviously, as well as on their way to their homes and on the way back from their homes to work – but the fact is is people are buying our furniture for their own homes simply because our tables and chairs are pleasant and convenient to use. Your chairs here for example are not well-made. That's why you have a slight stoop. Your

103

back has not been well supported. The stoop is slight now – sure – but if you go on sitting in chairs like this it will get more pronounced, and eventually you'll find you'll fold over and kind of collapse into yourself. You've probably seen elderly people whose faces are permanently turned towards the ground, and they have to use a stick or frame so they don't topple over? Well often that began with the kind of slight stoop you have, Paul, which, in the course of a few decades, became exponentially worse. The fact is, that the human head is incredibly heavy. The pressure it puts on the spine is an engineer's nightmare. In ten years' time you could find yourself recovering in hospital from surgery to your lower back. And however much they tell you the operation was a success and the titanium screws will take away the pain, you'll struggle, Paul, you'll struggle to even move. It's not just the weight of the head, it's the weight – well you know this better that I do – it's the weight of everything in it.

What? What is it?

Paul Nothing.

Tilman No. Say it.

Paul If I asked you to . . .

Tilman Mmm?

Paul If I asked you to . . .

If I asked you . . . to kiss me.

   Pause.

Tilman (*gently*) I'm not into the queer thing, Paul.

Paul Okay.

Tilman I'm not into it. I am *so* straight.

Paul Okay.

Tilman I'm not into the queer thing.

Paul Okay.

Tilman I'm boring – sorry – look at me: I'm like furniture.

But where are those *women*?

What are those women *doing*?

WOMEN WHERE ARE YOU?

Pause.

What?

Paul You mustn't think I'm . . .

Tilman What?

Paul That I am desperate for some kind of . . .

Or that I am unfaithful to Julia or . . .

I am content with my life.

Tilman Sure.

Paul I just want to make that clear to you.

Buzzer. Paul goes over.

Because this is not how we live.

Hello?

Women's laughter from the entryphone.

Hello?

Julia's Voice (*indistinct*) Paul?

Paul Hello? Hello?

Julia's Voice It's me. Forgotten my key.

More laughter from the women. He buzzes her in.

Tilman Not how you live?

Paul No. We don't live like this. We've never lived like this and we're not living like this now. Even when we could've lived like this, we didn't. (*Pause.*) You know, I should show you my studio.

Tilman Great.

Paul I keep my stuff there.

Tilman That's what? – your piano?

Paul No no – not piano. My machines –

Julia and Josefine enter mid-conversation, both in high spirits.

Julia . . . and of course the vast majority of people simply wanted to get on with their lives – but he had this idea it was a time of idealism – 'and of course we can shoot' et cetera et cetera – *

Josefine (*laughing*) Can you imagine me shooting someone?

Julia Ah but it was exactly the middle-class girls like you got the bankers' wives to open their doors –

Josefine You are such a bitch, Julia!

Julia I should've put that in the job-description – 'applicants must be pistol-ready'.

Josefine (*laughing*) Pistol-ready. This woman is completely mad.

Tilman So how was the shop?

Josefine How was the what?

Tilman The shop, the shop – you were going to the shop.

Julia Well we were on our way to the shop when Josefine said to me 'What's that?' so I said 'What's what?' and

* 'Und natürlich kann geschossen werden': from an interview with Ulrike Meinhof.

Josefine says to me 'Down there, down there.' And she's right – yes she is absolutely right – because down there is a staircase I have never even noticed, Paul, right under the shop selling all those lovely diaries and notebooks. And Josefine says to me 'Are you thinking what I'm thinking?' and I say 'Yes I probably am –'

Josefine One little drink.

Julia One little drink – which is odd because I never drink – neither of us ever drinks or even thinks about drinking – do we, Paul. But we go down the staircase and there is a bar with pretty paper lanterns and walls of exposed brick. So we sit at the bar and Josefine goes –

Josefine (*laughing*) I did not!

Julia (*laughing*) – goes – yes you did! – goes 'What we need is a whisky' – and before I can stop her she says to the barman: 'Two straight whiskies – set 'em up' – like she's some kind of cowboy –

Josefine Cowgirl – please.

Julia – some kind – exactly – of cowgirl. Then it's: 'Cheers – to the job.'

Josefine To the job.

Pause. Both women smile.

So after a couple more whiskies –

Julia Excuse me – who's telling this story?

So yes, after a few more whiskies Josefine starts in on this thing about how humble she feels at being given a job in my 'internationally renowned' department and how she's still 'reeling' as she puts it 'from the shock' and how delighted she is at being invited into my home in the middle of the night like this and getting to meet Paul in the middle of the night like this and then repeats herself a bit about how charming it is to meet such a stable and non-violent couple, it's so far from her own experience.

So I say to her, what d'you mean, shock? – of all the . . . the . . . the . . .

Josefine Cowgirls.

Julia Yes of all the cowgirls – thank you – who applied, you were the best candidate. And Josefine goes, 'Well yes that's the thing – I'd heard that you didn't like women.'

So I'm: 'Don't like women? Listen, Josefine, I have struggled for women, I have fought to give them power, I have shouted down and shamed my male colleagues in order to give the women of this university a voice.' But Josefine says – well I think this is what you said – says, 'Yes but promoting women isn't the same thing as liking them.' – Have I got this right?

Josefine (*nods*) Sure – sure – broadly speaking.

Julia Broadly speaking – okay.

So this is very interesting: 'What do you mean, Josefine, I don't like women?'

Tilman So you got to the shop?

Julia One moment, Mister Captain of Industry.

'What is it you've heard?' – I say to her. Well at that point Josefine clams right up – she clams right up and orders another whisky. Is that not so?

Pause.

Josefine (*nods*) And orders another whisky.

Julia Another very interesting thing is that Tilman here makes his own trousers. Yes she often wakes up in the middle of the night and finds him at work on the sewing-machine.

Paul I owe you an apology, Josefine.

Josefine What? No – not at all.

Paul I was thoughtless.

Josefine Not at all.

Paul Suicide is a terrible thing.

Josefine It's not important.

Paul She'd torn her blue-and-white towel into strips.

Josefine I'm just happy to be here, Paul.

Paul Your life's just beginning, but you don't realise that.

Josefine I think I do.

Paul That's all I was trying to say.

What?

Josefine I'm a bit drunk. I could punch you now.

Paul Go ahead.

She takes a swing at him. He blocks her.

Tilman Hey!

Paul Because boxing lifts people out of poverty and restores their self-respect. That's fine. You go ahead.

She takes another swing and punches his face.

Tilman No! Josefine!

Paul's face is bloody.

Paul (*calmly*) Get me some ice, would you?

Tilman Josefine!

Paul Get me some ice. Over there – the freezer.

Tilman goes to get ice.

You must train.

Josefine I train when I can, but I'm mostly in the library.

Paul Of course.

Josefine We've got this article to finish about Mantegna.

Paul Of course.

Josefine My field is Contemporary, but Julia is asking me to cover the Renaissance.

Tilman brings some ice etc.

Very gently he starts to wipe away the blood from Paul's face.

The women watch in silence.

Then –

Paul Of course then as now the United States of America was happy to incinerate small children.

Tilman Your lip is split just here.

Paul So what is perhaps surprising –

Ah – careful –

– is not that there was so much violence, but that there turned out to be so little. Thank you. Now give me the ice.

Julia What nation has not incinerated small children, Paul?

Paul Point taken, but – ah – ah –

He holds the ice over his mouth and nose and raises his other hand to show he can't speak.

Pause.

Tilman Is that your fridge humming?

They all listen.

FOUR

Josefine, Julia, Tilman – no Paul.

On the table now, a couple of bottles of alcohol, some pre-packed snacks, all unopened.

Tilman spins a coin on the table. It comes to rest, he spins it again.

Josefine Tilman?

The coin comes to rest. He spins it again.

Look at that: he is so desperate to smoke.

Tilman I am not.

The coin comes to rest. He spins it again.

Josefine Go out on the balcony – go on.

Tilman I do not smoke.

Josefine So what was that in your pocket?

Tilman In my pocket? No idea. It was a diagram.

Josefine On a cigarette packet.

Tilman No.

The coin comes to rest. He spins it again.

Josefine Show me. What diagram? Stop doing that!

Tilman No. Get off – off! OFF!

They struggle playfully. She kisses him. They kiss at length as if they were alone.

Then they have a whispered conversation, inaudible to the audience. Tilman is asking her to do something, she's refusing.

Tilman (*last words audible*) Go on. Ask her.

Josefine We were wondering . . . what Paul does.

Julia He makes dance music.

Josefine Dance music?

Julia Yes. He's very successful at it. You've probably danced to his music without realising. A lot of people have danced to his music – but when they meet him they have no idea. People have an image of the kind of man who makes dance music and Paul doesn't conform to it. And it's perfectly true that he himself doesn't dance – any more than I do – not in that way – not in the way you might – the complete surrender you described to a sense of well-being you can't really trust – the kind of dancing that goes on and on till daylight. But why not trust it if it gives you pleasure? Because I'm all for pleasure – I've nothing against pleasure – I simply don't experience it any more.

Tilman That can't be true. How can that be true?

Josefine He's always scribbling some diagram. I say to him, a table has four legs and a flat bit on top, that's not going to change, Tilman. Then he comes up – don't you – with some amazing idea that totally transforms the industry.

Tilman The folding table. The table with three legs. The table with no legs at all. NO NO DON'T HIT ME!

They all laugh to varying degrees.

But you must get pleasure from writing a book.

Julia Pleasure?

Tilman Or from – I don't know – finishing a book or . . .

Julia You think there is pleasure in finishing a book?

Tilman I don't know. Josefine says –

Julia Josefine says what?

Tilman Says you are an important author.

Julia Oh?

Tilman So you must get pleasure from your books, pleasure from writing – to be seen – for your name to be seen – to change the way people think –

Julia How they think about what?

Tilman I don't know, I don't know, it's not my domain, I only know what Josefine tells me, that you have changed the way people think about certain images – (*To Josefine.*) Isn't that what you said?

Julia Start a book and the problem is how do you finish it, finish a book and the problem is how do you start the next one.

Tilman Sure, sure – but all the same: to be an important author – come on, Josefine – help me!

Josefine Look at him – he's struggling – he's running out of things to say – he makes me laugh so much – why don't you just give up.

Tilman (*genial*) No! No! She can't say she gets no pleasure from what she does. It's unreasonable!

Josefine Tilman.

Tilman Well it's true!

What?

Josefine Stop it.

Julia Look – do help yourself to a drink, Tilman.

Tilman No thank you.

Josefine He doesn't.

Julia But I thought . . .

Josefine No – he won't – will you?

Tilman No.

Julia Then I don't understand why we went out and bought it.

Pause.

Josefine (*amused*) He's angry.

Tilman No I'm not.

Josefine He wishes he wasn't here.

Julia Oh? Is that true, Tilman?

Tilman No.

Josefine Liar.

Pause.

You are such a big fucking liar!

Julia Look, I'm sure all he wants to do is take care of you. He can see you're a little drunk and he'd probably – wouldn't you, Tilman – like to have you at home now – have you all wrapped up in bed. I mean I try and take care of the young women in my department but once they've left the building they are totally in the hands of others and what happens to them in the hands of others is none of my business – they can dance till the daylight comes – they can fuck till they're bruised inside – and if men want to take them home, if men want to wrap them up in bed, with just their heads poking out, I can understand that. Because I think I am right in saying that we women can go on, we can go on and on and on. Whereas men like to sleep. Is that not so, Tilman? It may be sex, it may be a stream of thought, but women can go on. Or it might be a screaming baby – not that I've ever had a screaming baby – God forbid I should ever have had a screaming baby and certainly I'll never – well look at me – because I'll never have a screaming baby now – but *had* I a screaming baby and it went on and on screaming in the night, I would offer it my breast. Unlike a man, I'd be awake for as long as my screaming baby needed me. Since a woman passes her baby from one breast to the other for as long as her baby needs her. Even if it means no sleep for her at all.

Josefine (*quietly, getting up*) Excuse me.

Tilman Josefine?

Josefine goes out on to the balcony, closing the door behind her.

Julia You must love her a great deal.

Pause.

Will she be alright out there?

Tilman I'm sorry?

Julia It's quite a drop.

(*Calls.*) Paul? Paul?

Tilman A drop?

Julia Off the edge, yes.

(*Calls.*) Paul? – will you come in here please?

Tilman What drop? It's a normal balcony.

Julia But she's drunk.

Tilman I don't think so.

Julia Then what is it 's wrong with her?

Tilman There's nothing wrong with her.

Paul appears, barefoot.

Julia Look at this: he's changed his shirt.

Paul (*looking at Tilman*) Yes I had blood on the . . .

Julia Would you see if Josefine is alright? Tilman is worried about her.

Tilman Of course she's alright.

Julia Paul? I'm talking to you.

Paul Sure.

Paul goes out on to the balcony.

He and Josefine can be seen beginning a conversation.

Julia I haven't seen that shirt of his for years.

Tilman (*soft and intense*) Want to know last year's pre-tax profits? – three and a half million euros. Sure there's tax, sure there is re-investment – but all the same that's three and a half million euros in the hands of a piece of shit like me.

Outside, Josefine and Paul can be seen laughing – she touches his nose.

Because you say 'love her' as if it's some kind of of of mental illness that I have. But my point is is I would give away all that money just like that to spend one hour of my life with her.

Julia It's simply that the balcony is dangerous.

Tilman Yea – yea – is dangerous.

Julia You didn't see how much she drank.

Tilman How much she drank – sure – and listen: it's not that I dislike you.

Julia . . .

Tilman You and Paul – I like you both – I like this . . . atmosphere you have – I like the Greek salad thing that's going on here – great. (*Smiles*) I'm simply warning you.

Julia You're warning me?

Tilman While I have – yes, warning you – while I have this opportunity.

Pause. Outside, Josefine and Paul now deep in conversation.

Julia So Josefine's worth three million euros.

Tilman I beg your pardon?

Julia You're telling me she's worth three million euros? What would you get then for four or five?

Tilman Look, I appreciate that you have fought for women, all I am saying is do not fight for mine.

What?

Julia (*amused*) You look like you want to hit me.

Tilman I do not want to hit you.

Julia What is it you want to do to me then, Tilman?

Tilman Because you know nothing about Josefine.

Julia So what is it you want to do?

Oh? – nothing? – so what is there to know?

Tilman Exactly: we are employers – employers keep their distance.

Julia And if she wants to talk to me? – to take me to a bar and talk to me?

Tilman She does not want to talk to you. She does not want to take you to a bar and talk to you – and even if she *does* take you to a bar and talk to you she has nothing to talk to you *about*.

Josefine comes back in. She's holding Paul's hand and pulling him into the room.

Josefine He's promised he'll play us one of his tracks.

Paul (*good-humoured*) No no – I did not promise – nobody wants to hear that kind of music – it's just made by machines – I . . .

Josefine Come on. You said. Look at him: he's not even wearing shoes. DANCE! DANCE!

Paul Another time.

Josefine (*to Tilman*) You can actually *see* the pumping station – such an amazing view. Make him, Tilman.

Tilman Make him what?

Josefine 'Make him what?' Make him play us his music.

Tilman We ought to go now.

Josefine No. No. We're staying!

Paul?

Paul goes over to the music system and, using headphones, cues up a tape on a reel-to-reel tape-recorder.

You see – you see – he promised.

Paul takes off the headphones and presses play. Soft and melancholy music: Beethoven, final Bagatelle in B flat from Op. 119.

What's that?

They listen.

No that's too sad. Stop it.

They listen.

This isn't dance music. Stop it.

They listen.

Julia (*softly*) Turn off the music, Paul.

Midway through the passage of gently climbing semiquavers Paul turns off the music.

Tilman looks at him and claps softly seventeen times.

Pause.

Josefine I don't understand what's happening.

FIVE

Josefine, Julia, Tilman, Paul.

Paul with the tone of a relaxed and confident raconteur.

Paul I was unbearable when I was seven or eight years old. Well I'm unbearable now – who isn't unbearable? – but back then I was unbearable in a completely different way. We lived in a communal building and my parents were political, they were out a lot confronting, obviously, the police, and I was conceived on a mattress on the floor – or that's what my father said. My mother abandoned me for political reasons: and it's true that even at the age of seven or eight I polished my shoes and was insufferably bourgeois. I still am, pretty much. But my father gave up on the revolution, got a job in the rapidly growing field of computer sciences, and supported me. Our new apartment had tall west-facing windows with trees outside. It had a floor I could slide across in socks. The piano came up in its piano-shoe and the four men who carried it petted me – they were sincere and wore blue overalls. Thus I was able to continue my studies until – as I was explaining earlier on to Tilman – until the day I discovered that due to a genetic defect I had no soul. Well! Nobody had ever told me this! I felt like the boy at school who's spent the whole day with a notice pinned to his back saying 'kick me' – and not even his so-called friends have bothered to tell him, so exquisite is the joke.

I will pass over in silence the self-pity and self-hatred that followed – even if descriptions of private insanity and deliberate self-harm are what pass these days as tragic. Suffice to say, one summer on the island of Thasos – 'crowned' as the poet says 'with forests' and lying off the sea close to the ancient goldmines of Kavala – I met Julia, and in the way of young people everywhere we devoured each other.

Not long after that we bought these uncomfortable chairs – and have been sitting on them ever since.

Julia Would you leave your baby, Josefine?

Josefine What? I don't know. I don't have a baby.

Julia But if you did – if you did have a baby.

Tilman Well of course not.

Julia Oh?

Tilman Why would she leave her baby?

Julia Paul's mother did.

Tilman Why would she leave her baby? She doesn't have a baby. It wouldn't be *her* baby.

Julia Whose baby would it be then?

Tilman It would be ours – it would be our baby.

Paul Yes of course it would – he's right – it wouldn't be her baby – it would be theirs.

Pause.

Tilman West-facing.

Paul Sorry? Yes.

Tilman So you got the sunset.

Paul Sure – well – yes – no – the sun was setting but you couldn't see it.

Tilman But you knew – even as a little boy you knew it was going down.

Paul Yes – oh yes – it was going down behind the buildings opposite. The sky changed colour.

Julia She could still leave it.

Tilman Sure – but she wouldn't want to.

Josefine I might, Tilman – I might have a baby and want to leave it – I don't know *how* I'd feel – you can't rule it out.

Paul I should just say: I wasn't a baby.

Josefine You can't rule it out – you can't speak *for* me.

Tilman (*conciliatory*) I know that. Forgive me.

Josefine You don't know what kind of mother I'd be.

Tilman (*as before*) I accept that.

Josefine Don't speak *for* me. Please.

Tilman (*as before*) Sure.

Josefine In front of people. It's . . .

Tilman (*as before*) Humiliating. I'm sorry.

Josefine You don't even *want* a baby – he thinks a baby would be like him – something wrong with its mind – but there's nothing wrong with his mind – the only thing wrong with his mind is he thinks there's something wrong with it.

Tilman (*as before*) Sure.

Josefine Which there is not, Tilman.

Tilman (*as before*) Sure.

Josefine Because maybe Paul's mother was right to leave him – I'm sorry, Paul, but maybe she was – maybe she needed to . . . I don't know . . . be free. Maybe it was necessary.

Tilman Piano-shoe – what's that?

Paul It's a device for moving a piano.

Tilman Okay. Interesting.

Josefine Do you mind that I'm having a baby, Tilman?

Pause. Tilman starts to absorb this.

Julia said I must tell you.

Pause. Tilman continues to absorb the information.

Paul Congratulations.

Josefine Thank you.

Tilman?

Look at him: he can't think what to say.

(*Amused.*) Julia was quite stern with me. 'Why aren't you telling him? What are you scared of?' Tilman?

Tilman (*inward*) Sure you can go into a shop and you can buy some trousers –

122

Josefine Tilman?

Tilman – and you can try the trousers on in the shop and see what they look like in front of a mirror and the trousers will probably look okay –

Josefine Tilman? – do you want to go home?

Tilman – but when you look more closely – no, I am fine – look more closely at the trousers – at the seams of the trousers – and when you reverse the pockets and look at the way the white pockets are stitched into the fabric then you start thinking: well I could do this myself – I could stitch these pockets into the fabric myself – I could create these seams.

Slight pause.

Paul Sure, I can understand that – but the thing is, Tilman –

Tilman The thing is *what*? The thing is *what*? (*To Julia.*) Why did you make her drink?

Josefine She didn't make me drink, Tilman.

Tilman WHY DID YOU MAKE HER DRINK?

Josefine (*very softly, restraining him*) Hey. Hey. Less aggressive, please. Tilman.

She holds him and kisses his face.

(*As before.*) Hey. It was only a little whisky. Be calm. We're having a baby – it's good, it's good.

Pause.

Julia She asked me to drink with her, Tilman. All this fuss about alcohol – all this concern about coffee –

Josefine (*softly*) Come on, come on. I was going to tell you. Come on.

Julia – don't you see – they're just new forms of control –

Josefine (*softly*) Say that you love me. Tilman – say that you love me.

A phone starts to buzz.

Julia And whenever a woman escapes one form of control, another is immediately invented.

Paul I'm sure Josefine knows that.

Julia I'm not so convinced, Paul.

She picks up the phone.

(*Brightly.*) Marko! Hi! (*Moving away.*) No, no – not disturbing me at all – we're just having a little party – no, no – go ahead, Marko, tell me –

She goes out.

Josefine (*softly*) Tilman. Come on. Say that you love me. Hey.

Paul turns on the tap and lets the water run over his hand.

Paul You mustn't dislike Julia. I'll tell you: the pile of applications stacked up there on that table – it was enormous. And of all the young women who applied – and young men too – you were the one she selected. Sure, she comes out with the 'no free-will' bullshit, but over a decision like this she'll agonise and agonise.

Yes at first your name will be in pretty small print and hers will be huge on articles you have largely written yourself – and at her request. But in just a few years you'll contribute to catalogues, you'll be on the phone to people like Marko – artists worth millions – you'll be flying . . . I don't know . . . flying to Venice, flying to Beijing.

Paul continues to turn his hand in the stream of water.

The baby will hold you back. In fact it will hold back the work of the whole department, that's why she's angry. But you mustn't dislike her: she's selected you.

Josefine I do not dislike her.

Paul This is getting quite cold now. (*The water.*)

Josefine I do not dislike her, but would you please stop talking.

Paul Sure. Stop talking. Sure.

Josefine Thank you.

Paul I'm happy to stop talking.

Josefine Thank you. It's not that I don't like you talking.

Paul Sure.

Josefine I'd just like you to stop.

Paul Tilman thinks in another ten years I'll struggle to move.

Josefine Please.

Paul Because of the way I sit.

He turns off the tap and dries his hand. At the same time Tilman gently takes hold of one of the bottles.

Josefine (*softly*) Come on, Tilman. Look at my eyes. What colour are my eyes? That's right. Look at me.

Tilman Dr Haas made me a proposition earlier – didn't you, Dr Haas.

Josefine (*softly*) If you want to go, you can – we don't have to stay.

Tilman Invited me to look round his studio. Where is your studio, Dr Haas?

Paul Couple of blocks away. It's on Schützenstrasse.

Tilman Yea yea – Schützenstrasse. That's where his machines are. (*He smiles.*)

Josefine What? What?

Tilman You really smashed his face.

> *He gently opens one of the bottles and pours himself a drink. He downs it and pours another.*

Rabbi . . . Priest . . . Yea I'd like people to come to me and for them to say: 'Guide me, Tilman – I can't find my way from the bed to the bathroom. I keep banging into the bedroom wall.'

> *He downs the drink and pushes his face against Josefine's stomach. She strokes his head.*

Josefine You see how much he loves me, Paul. Who wouldn't want to be protected by this man? – Who wouldn't want to be wrapped up by Tilman and put to bed? – or kissed by him. Look at him: he's so sure there's something wrong with his mind, but I say to him, Tilman, I'm not interested in your mind, I'm interested in your body, he thinks that's funny, he doesn't like his body, he hates mirrors, he'd love to have a cigarette, but now he can't, he really can't, I'm not going to let him, he's just too beautiful, plus going to be a father now. What're you doing, Tilman? (*Amused.*) Stop it. He's pushing with his face, he thinks he can see right into me, he thinks he can see my uterus, you're trying to see my uterus, aren't you – aren't you – stop pushing me with your face like that, he's like a dog – behave! – Tilman!

Tell you what, you should get him to dance for you – get him to dance to your dance music – at home he goes mad – he dances from room to room –

> *Tilman has started to undo her trousers.*

No. Stop that. Stop that now. Stop it. HEY!

She slaps his head hard and pushes him away.

(*With new intensity.*) We've got so many rooms and he
dances all through them, but the thing is, Paul, is I'm not
some kind of child, I know that my life is ahead of me,
I don't need to be told that, I don't need to be told that
I smile like Ulrike Meinhof, you don't need to make me
think about ideology and death, I think every day about
ideology and death – Julia too, we can't help it, we like
it – ideology and death – it's our domain. And look,
what d'you want a soul for, Paul? – who needs a soul? –
what is this thing about souls? – he's just as bad – look
at him – becoming a priest, what is he talking about?
Because Julia's right – the world's a material fact, get
over it.

Paul Sure.

Tilman He looks like he's going to cry.

Josefine What?

Tilman Look at him: he looks like he's going to cry.

Paul I'm not going to cry. What am I going to cry
about?

Tilman Why are you making Paul cry, Josefine?

Josefine I'm not. (*She does up her trousers*) Paul doesn't
like me, that's all. That's fine: I don't need to be liked,
but I do ask to be respected. The funny thing is, Paul,
is men your age are normally all over me but you're not
over me at all. I appreciate that – and please, I'm not
meaning to be unkind.

Paul I'll get him to do that, then.

Josefine Mmm?

Paul I'll get him to dance for me.

Josefine (*brightly*) Yes! Yes! You must!

Julia comes back in.

Julia Oh? – Must what?

Josefine Make Tilman dance – he has to.

Julia Dance – hmm – sure – (*To Paul.*) That's Marko, he's calling me from Los Angeles, they're giving him a show and do I remember the piece I wrote for Kassel? – sure Marko d'you know what time it is? – he's somewhere in Santa Monica, late afternoon he thinks – no I mean here Marko, the time here in Germany – can I adapt it? – can I adapt what? – well the piece that you wrote for Kassel – sure just give me a couple of weeks – couple of weeks no I need it for Monday, I need you to take out Schwarzkogler, I want you to cut out Schwarzkogler for Monday – what d'you mean Marko cut out Schwarzkogler for Monday? – just take them out, just take out Schwarzkogler and Mühl – Mühl too? – yes take them out – you want me to take out Schwarzkogler *and* Mühl? – I don't know – you don't *know* but you just told me to take them out – yes take out Mühl, obviously take out Mühl, but maybe Schwarzkogler's important, maybe if you take out Schwarzkogler there'll be no context for my work – but listen Marko you *called* me to take out Schwarzkogler, the whole purpose of this call was to get me to take out Schwarzkogler and now you're telling me that Schwarzkogler's back in – don't shout at me – I'm not – don't shout at me – I'm not shouting at you Marko – I hate it here – oh do you Marko – I hate it by the beach I hate the sun – well Marko if you hate the sun and hate it by the beach why did you accept to go to California? – just take out Schwarzkogler – why have you surrendered to your your your your whatever the word is vanity – okay I'm sorry

just take out Schwarzkogler – you mean not Mühl – not
Mühl just Schwarzkogler – no Marko I cannot take out
Schwarzkogler, I cannot take out Mühl, I cannot change
what I write to satisfy every artist's vanity and certainly
not by Monday, and in fact no, not at all, not ever, it
will destroy my argument – I don't give a shit, says
Marko, Julia, about you and your academic argument,
just take them out, just take the fuckers out.

> *Pause. Julia's phone starts to buzz. They all go quiet,
> as if the person calling might hear them. Eventually it
> stops.*

(*Smiles.*) Know what, we ought to celebrate. What d'you
say, Tilman – how does it feel to be a father?

Tilman Feels great.

Julia Potential father.

Tilman Feels really great. (*Downs another drink.*)

Julia We ought to open the champagne. Paul?

Paul What?

Julia We ought to open the champagne.

Paul There's no champagne – there's only that. (*The
alcohol on the table.*)

Julia 'There's only that' – okay – is it my fault 'there's
only that'?

Paul Well yes, Julia – it is.

Julia He's right of course – there's not much in this
house – I'm sorry, Josefine –

Josefine We don't mind.

Julia There's me, there's Paul, there's really not much
else – my books, his old tapes of course – but really not

129

much else – not even in the fridge – well, as you've seen. We tend not to keep things – do you keep things, Tilman? – do you collect?

Tilman Collect what? Sure – some things.

Julia Oh? – what things do you collect?

Tilman This and that.

Julia I thought he didn't drink.

Tilman I'm sorry?

Julia Thought you didn't drink – you said that he didn't drink.

Josefine I like it when he drinks – it makes him funny.

Julia Funny – sure – but what is it you collect then, Tilman? Perhaps he collects women!

Tilman I don't think so.

Josefine (*to Julia*) Don't say that.

Julia Then maybe he collects men – what is it you collect, Tilman?

Tilman downs another drink, and pours another.

(*To Paul.*) You know he's issued me a warning?

Josefine What warning? No he hasn't. Tilman?

Paul Of course he hasn't issued you a warning. Warning about what?

Julia (*to Josefine*) Oh by the way, if Marko calls again, you talk to him.

Josefine I don't know Marko – I've never met him.

Julia Never met him – sure – but he knows you. I told him: I've a new young woman works for me – and he goes: 'Is she hot?'

Paul Of course he hasn't issued you a warning.

Julia 'Is she hot?' – That is the level, Josefine, of discourse among men.

Paul Of course he hasn't issued you a warning. Julia?

Julia (*with deep vehemence*) Because I tell you something: sooner than hang a Marko I'd rather spit on that wall.

Long pause.

Paul goes over and touches her.

Paul (*gently*) Of course he hasn't issued you a warning.

Julia Oh look at this: he's touching me.

Tilman Paul. Paul.

Paul Mmm? What?

Tilman Play us your music, Paul.

Josefine Yes, yes, play us your music.

Tilman We want to hear the machines.

Josefine That's right – the machines! – come on!

Paul moves away from Julia. He operates a remote.

Dance music.

They listen.

Is this really one of yours?

Paul Produced it – yes.

Josefine Amazing!

Paul Not 'mine', but I produced it.

Josefine What?

Paul I said not 'mine', but I produced it.

Josefine Tilman! – he produced this!

Tilman Sure.

He downs a drink and pours another. They all listen to the insistent rhythm.

Josefine Now Tilman's going to dance.

Come on, Tilman – show them!

We've got so many rooms, he dances through all of them – they all join up.

Come on, Tilman – on your feet!

That's the second bottle, he's going to be so hungover.

Music continues. Tilman gets to his feet.

That's it! That's it! Show them!

Tilman dances. They all watch. After a while:

Have you ever hit a woman, Paul?

Paul No.

Josefine What?

Paul No. Of course not. Why're you asking me that?

Josefine 'Of course not' – You're such a gentleman. Paul's such a gentleman, Tilman. He'd never hit a woman – especially not a pregnant one!

Tilman dances.

See? – that's what he does at home. Show them from room to room, Tilman.

As Tilman goes on dancing, he begins to repeat some of the vocal samples on the track.

Tilman (*inward*) . . . Hold me . . . touch me . . . touch me . . .

Josefine I said show them from room to room.

Tilman gravitates towards the balcony.

(*Laughing.*) No, not that, that's the balcony.

He's so drunk.

Tilman, that is the balcony.

That is the balcony, Tilman – come back inside.

Out on the balcony Tilman climbs on to a table or some other structure.

Don't. You're being frightening now.

Turn off the music, Paul.

Don't. Tilman. No! YOU'RE BEING FRIGHTENING!

Paul turns off the music.

(*Gently.*) Tilman, come down.

Now come back inside.

In the silence, Julia's phone is buzzing. She looks at it and holds it out to Josefine.

Julia Josefine?

Josefine (*to Tilman*) You mustn't frighten everyone like that. (*Taking the phone.*) Hello? Julia's phone.

. . .

No, I'm afraid she's not available.

. . .

Josefine . . . Her assistant, yes.

. . .

Party? It's not really a party, it's more a kind of a . . .

. . .

Why're you asking me *that?*

. . .

Alright, alright, I'm twenty-four.

(*Sotto.*) Why is he / asking me that?

Julia I never said party, I wouldn't call / this a party.

Josefine Of course I've heard of you, I've studied your work, / everyone has –

Paul Of course it's a party. It has the ingredients of a party.

Julia But just because it has / the ingredients . . .

Josefine (*glancing at Julia*) That's really a personal thing, it's not something I'm going to talk about right now. (*Laughs*) Well thank you, thank you, / it's kind of you to say that.

Julia It may have the ingredients, Paul, but that doesn't make it a party.

Paul (*genial*) Well I / disagree.

Josefine Okay, but I think Julia's already spoken to you about that, I can't make that decision for her – / hey – Tilman –

She tries to take his hand.

Paul I disagree: there's music, dancing, conversation –

Julia Conversation?

Josefine Hey – Tilman –

She tries again to take his hand.

Julia Conversation? No.

She watches Josefine.

Josefine Look, I understand that you're concerned about this, but . . . Uh-huh . . . Uh-huh . . . Yes of course / I'm listening . . .

Julia No one's having a conversation.

Paul We're having a conversation now.

Julia No we're not, Paul.

Josefine – do not agree / to anything.

Tilman (*mumbles inaudibly*) Your eyes . . .

Josefine The best thing is, is I will pass all this on to Julia. (*To Tilman.*) What's that?

Tilman (*mumbles more distinctly*) Your eyes . . . are pink.

Josefine Mmm?

Tilman Your eyes . . . are pink.

Josefine They're what? (*To phone.*) Sorry, look, I'm going to have to ask Julia to call you back in the morning.

. . .

No, sorry, I can't do that, I have to go.

She terminates the call.

Of course my eyes aren't pink, Tilman, they're the colour / they always are.

Julia You didn't agree to anything, did you?

Josefine What? No.

Julia Good.

Josefine They're the colour they always are, Tilman – don't look at me like that. I'm going to take you home.

Julia Take him home? – but I thought we were going / to work.

Tilman But Paul – have you ever hit / a *man*?

Josefine Work?

Paul Hit a man?

Julia That's what we said – yes?

Josefine I don't remember.

Tilman (*simultaneous with previous line*) Yes – hit a man. Have you?

Paul Of course I've hit a man. I hit men / all the time.

Josefine Really? – I don't remember – work?

Tilman begins slowly moving towards Paul.

Tilman Hit me now then.

Paul I slam them into walls. I bounce men off parked cars. I throw them to the ground and kick them.

Tilman So hit me now.

Josefine What're you doing, Tilman? That's enough.

Paul I head-butt strangers. I grab men by the arms and bite them.

Josefine Tilman.

Paul Once I've got them against the ropes, I pummel and pummel their faces. I crack their eye-sockets.

Tilman Yea – yea – you pummel them.

Josefine That's enough, Tilman. (*to Julia*) Please make them stop.

Paul I bend back men's fingers and snap them. I can blind a man with one quick jab –

Tilman One quick jab – sure.

Josefine Please . . .

Paul I'm waiting for him on the concrete steps. The moment he appears, I'm on him, and I break his skull.

Josefine No: make them stop!

Tilman has completed his journey towards Paul, and now puts his arms around him as if he needs Paul's support to keep standing.

Tilman So hit me now.

The two men sway together. Paul raises his arms as if to say 'This has nothing to do with me'.

Beethoven: the Bagatelle resumes at the climbing semi-quavers. The high tessitura makes the swaying men appear almost like figures on the top of a musical box.

Lights fade to black, but the music completes, giving way to tape-hiss.

SIX

Julia on her own. Her computer is open on the table, she's changed her clothes, she's made some coffee. She sips the coffee, lost in thought.

Josefine appears.

Julia Coffee?

Josefine makes sound of assent.

Julia pours coffee.

Josefine Already working.

Julia Have to.

Josefine Quite light now. What's the time?

Julia Sevenish.

Josefine Sevenish. Oh.

Pause.

I think I'll . . .

Julia Oh?

Josefine Yes, think I'll go outside a moment.

Julia Sure. It's cold. You'll get cold arms. Wear this.

Josefine Mmm?

Julia It will cover your arms.

She gives Josefine an item of clothing. Josefine puts it on, maybe Julia helps.

She laughs.

Josefine (*genial*) What?

Julia Nothing. Ten minutes, please.

Josefine Ten minutes what?

Julia I need your help. Would you?

Josefine Of course.

Josefine goes out on to the balcony.

Julia sits in front of her computer, puts on her glasses, types a little, removes her glasses, moves to the sink. She gags as if she might be sick, but resists being sick. She gets a glass, turns on the cold tap, holds her hand under the water, waits, puts down the glass, turns the tap off, dries her hands, goes back to her computer.

She puts her glasses back on and starts to type again.

She removes her glasses and sits back: she bites her lip, clearly haunted by an internal struggle.

She gets up again, gets painkillers from a blister-pack, swallows the painkillers with her coffee.

Josefine comes back in.

Josefine You're right – it's cold out there. Sun's coming up – must be behind those buildings.

Julia It comes up every morning, Josefine.

Pause.

Josefine, would you read out to me that paragraph.

Josefine Sure.

She sits at the computer.

'The persistent traces' – this one?

Julia nods.

'The persistent traces of overwhelming violence, ghostly aftershocks of representation itself, recall the staged fantasies of Schwarzkogler; whilst the erasure of the female body owes an obvious debt to Mühl's early "actions" in Vienna. But the artist's unique voice is not in question –'

Julia Thank you.

Would you like more coffee, Josefine?

Josefine I'd quite like to go home now.

Julia Of course: if we could just do this first.

Josefine Sure. Do what?

Julia Take out Schwarzkogler and Mühl.

Josefine (*after a pause*) But I thought –

Julia Oh? Thought what? Just take them out please.

She watches as Josefine prepares to type.

Josefine I can't do this.

Julia (*genial*) Why not, Josefine? – yes you can – of course you can.

Again, Josefine prepares to type, but pauses.

You do want a career?

Josefine A career?

Julia Because if you want a career you will have to learn, I'm afraid, to be reliable.

Josefine Reliable?

Julia If you want to have access to the artists.

Josefine I don't understand what you mean.

Julia I think you do, Josefine.

Pause.

Josefine But you can't change your whole argument just to / suit the –

Julia (*genial*) I think I'm probably the best judge of what I can or cannot change. Just take them out. I don't think it will be so difficult.

Julia watches as Josefine types.

(*Gently.*) Take your time.

Julia watches as Josefine completes the task.

Okay? (*Josefine nods.*) How does it read now?

Josefine 'Persistent traces of overwhelming violence – ghostly aftershocks of representation itself – the artist's unique voice is not in question.'

Julia Good.

Josefine 'Marko tightens the noose of history around the viewer's neck.'

Julia Good. Excellent. Scroll down please to the next reference.

Pause.

What?

Josefine He knew that I was pregnant.

Julia Marko?

Josefine How did he know that I was pregnant?

Julia Well I told him of course.

Josefine Why did you tell him that?

Julia We really do need to finish this.

Josefine Why did you tell him?

Julia He likes to feel a connection – you'll see.

Josefine See what?

Julia You'll be in his mind now. He'll answer your calls, he'll think of you when he needs something done. For example, this article.

Josefine I don't want to be 'in his mind'.

Julia Yes you do, Josefine – you do want to be in his mind – it's just that you haven't realised. Now scroll down to the next reference please.

Josefine scrolls down.

Josefine (*after a pause*) Have you seen Tilman?

Julia Tilman is asleep.

Josefine Oh?

Julia Well obviously. Yes.

What is the next reference?

Josefine Just that I haven't seen him.

Julia I closed the door. You probably walked straight past.

Pause.

Found it yet?

Josefine Here – here – 'the influence of Mühl' –

Julia Exactly. Change it.

Josefine But this bit is important.

Julia Change it, Josefine.

Pause. Josefine types.

That colour suits you.

Josefine When did they get back?

Julia You've changed that?

Josefine Yes.

Julia Good. Then find the next one.

Josefine So when did the two of them get back?

Julia From Schützenstrasse? I've really no idea.

What is the next one?

Pause.

Josefine turns to look at Julia.

Josefine Are you alright?

Julia I have a headache. You? Not sick or anything?

Josefine Sick? (*Realises.*) No, no – thank you – no, not sick at all. I'm feeling good.

So Paul was with him?

Julia I imagine.

Josefine Ah, here's another thing about –

Julia Delete it.

Josefine It won't make sense if I just –

Julia Delete it. We'll make sense of it later.

Josefine types.

I imagine Paul was with him, yes – he wouldn't've got back into the building otherwise.

Josefine stops typing and makes to get up.

Josefine I'm wondering if I should go and –

Julia Let's just work now shall we, Josefine, while we can.

Josefine Okay.

Julia I've told you: I've closed the door.

Josefine Okay.

Julia I'd rather we weren't disturbed.

Josefine Okay.

I would quite like to go home soon.

Julia Of course.

Josefine I don't feel very clean.

Julia Of course, I understand, let's just complete this shall we?

Josefine Sure.

Julia I don't think it will take much longer.

Pause.

You were an outstanding candidate.

Josefine Thank you.

Julia I can say that now.

Josefine Thank you – you did already say.

Julia Well I'm saying it again.

Pause.

Josefine Thank you.

Julia Did you delete the footnotes?

Josefine Mmm? – the footnotes? – no.

Julia Find and delete the related footnotes.

Josefine types in silence.
She stops after a while and stares into space.

Is there a problem?

Josefine No.

Josefine resumes typing.

To help in the playing of Scene Five, Marko's side of the phone-call is suggested here. His voice may be faintly audible in performance, but should not be intelligible to the audience.

Josefine Hello? Julia's phone.

Marko Can I speak to Julia, please.

Josefine No, I'm afraid she's not available.

Marko Who is this?

Josefine Josefine.

Marko Ah – the assistant.

Josefine Her assistant, yes.

Marko I hear that you're having a party.

Josefine Party? It's not really a party, it's more a kind of a . . .

Marko How old are you, Josefine?

Josefine Why're you asking me *that*?

Marko Just curious. Not a secret is it?

Josefine Alright, alright, I'm twenty-four.

(*Sotto.*) Why is he asking me that?

Marko Just some of you bright young things have never heard of me.

Josefine Of course I've heard of you, I've studied your work, everyone has –

Marko But listen – I also hear that you're having a baby.

Josefine (*glancing at Julia*) That's really a personal thing, it's not something I'm going to talk about right now.

Marko Just wanted to say fantastic.

Josefine (*laughs*) Well thank you, thank you, it's kind of you to say that.

Marko You know that I need some work done on my catalogue here.

Josefine Okay, but I think Julia's already spoken to you about that, I can't make that decision for her – hey – Tilman –

She tries to take his hand.

Marko I've got a real problem with the way my work is being represented. Plus these Californians are so fucking ignorant –

Josefine Hey – Tilman –

She tries again to take his hand.

Marko It's all this 'abstract expressionism' bullshit.

Josefine Look, I understand that you're concerned about this, but . . .

Marko Total bullshit.

Josefine Uh-huh.

Marko With me?

Josefine Uh-huh.

Marko Are you listening to what I'm saying?

Josefine Yes of course I'm listening.

Marko I don't want to hear this abstract expressionism bullshit *plus* I don't want those Viennese fuckers anywhere near my work. Is that understood?

Tilman (*mumbles inaudibly*) Your eyes . . .

Josefine The best thing is, is I will pass all this on to Julia. (*To Tilman.*) What's that?

Marko (*to Josefine's next cue*) She already knows this. This is not about her – it's my work we're talking about.

Tilman (*mumbles more distinctly*) Your eyes . . . are pink.

Josefine Mmm?

Tilman Your eyes . . . are pink.

Josefine They're what? (*To phone.*) Sorry, look, I'm going to have to ask Julia to call you back in the morning.

Marko No you tell her I need to speak to her *now*.

Josefine No, sorry, I can't do that, I have to go.

She terminates the call.